SILKSCREEN PRINTING

IN THE HOME STUDIO

Advanced
HAVOLINE
MOTOR OIL
Spray Mount
FLOUR

Angela Hall

SILKSCREEN PRINTING
IN THE HOME STUDIO

THE CROWOOD PRESS

CONTENTS

INTRODUCTION

Silkscreen printing is one of the most accessible and fun forms of reproducing a design using simple equipment and materials. The 'screen' is a piece of mesh, tightly stretched over a frame and a print is quickly created by pushing a thin film of ink through a stencil placed over the fine weave onto paper. Whether using simple paper or photographic stencils, the process is the same, transmitting ink evenly through the open areas of the design.

The method gives a positive representation unlike other printing techniques such as etching, woodcut and lino. You are always working the 'right way' around and it is easy to view your design without having to imagine how it will work when reversed. Purpose-built presses and elaborate inking techniques are not required and a printing space can be set up and easily dismantled and stored.

Before I started writing this book, I imagined that describing a process I had been using for many years would be straight forward and that I would be able to easily condense my knowledge into a clear and user-friendly guide. Little did I know that when I started to unpick my working methods, I would discover countless alternative ways of achieving the same result.

This book is aimed at demystifying and simplifying the silkscreen process, making it accessible outside of a professional print studio but giving the learner the step-by-step skills to use a more professional set-up in the future. It will focus on how to create a small home set-up making use of existing household equipment.

Each chapter is a collection of skills, inspiration and basic know-how, which you can dip into from different levels and test your knowledge through the many projects that are explored within the chapters. It begins by giving an insight into developing print expertise with basic equipment and materials. It then takes the reader on a printing adventure that includes home set-up, designing for print and a chapter-by-chapter explanation of basic techniques. It will enable the user to start printing from the outset as well as experimenting with the many creative possibilities the technique offers and how to troubleshoot any problems that might arise.

There is an in-depth exploration into basic hand-cut paper stencils, expressive monoprinting and finally photo silkscreen printing. If the reader has some experience already they may find new ways of working with the process. There is also a section on creating digital artwork using a range of free apps and an introduction to basic software and print output. Although I am not a major user of digital techniques in the creation of my work, I surprised myself with how easy it was to manipulate images, create better layouts and incorporate text.

As a naturally inquisitive person I spent a lot of time researching practical methods alongside my own creative practice. I tested and experimented with 'new to me' techniques and struggled at first with things that I thought would be difficult, only to find that I had acquired a more helpful way of bringing my prints to fruition.

I have included all my trials and investigations within the book and hope that they will provide a starting point for your print discoveries.

CHAPTER 1

EQUIPMENT AND MATERIALS

All printmaking activities are messy, and involve specialised tools, inky mixtures, cleaning liquids and stacks of paper. Silkscreen printing is no exception and can seem like an unlikely activity to embark on in the kitchen or bedroom, but if you limit resources and print size, it's perfectly feasible with a bit of planning.

Most silkscreen printing equipment has a narrow profile and lies flat, and can be stored under the bed or placed against a wall or in a shed or garage. Screens are light and easy to move around too, and easy to stack together when not in use.

My first piece of advice is to avoid the temptation to invest in huge amounts of kit when starting out. It's not necessary to buy everything that is mentioned in this chapter and better if you invest in quality basics such as screens and squeegees that will last for years of printing if properly cared for. Maintaining a realistic approach is important and it is essential to decide on what size of space you will be working in and find equipment that can be used efficiently and easily cleaned and stored. Be considerate when using your workspace too, especially when shared with others in a home environment.

It is recommended that beginners start with an A4 printing area to learn the basics. As you progress through the chapters and gain more experience you can progress to larger screens and print space. Screens are attached to a printing board that is larger than the screen size: you may want to consider future-proofing and get one that can accommodate larger screens and is suitable for printing up to A3 and A2. I suggest that you start with a simple set-up and add supplies as you gain in confidence and experience.

All equipment and materials used throughout this book and listed within this chapter can be sourced online or found in the home. A list of preferred suppliers is contained in the appendix and is a good way to get started; however, used and second-hand equipment can be readily found. A word of warning, though, if you are inexperienced I would only purchase new screens if you are not familiar with mesh size or where screens are damaged or stained.

The photo-silkscreen process is covered in more detail in Chapter 5 and requires a lightbox and UV light source. I have provided an overview of this equipment and associated materials in this chapter too.

All tools and supplies listed in this chapter are suitable for getting started with silkscreen, but the list is not definitive and you will start to add your own favourite products and handmade items.

Silkscreen printing requires a washing area for cleaning the screen at the end of the printing process to remove stubborn ink, photo stencils and so on. This can be in a sink or using an outside hosepipe, but it's important to decide where you are going to clean your equipment from the start. Simple monoprinting and paper stencils are easily cleaned using a bucket of water, so you don't always need to be near a sink.

Ink can be stored in a range of containers with tight-fitting lids.

HEALTH AND SAFETY EQUIPMENT

The main health and safety requirements within a home print set-up are related to the materials you will be using, the area you have set aside to print and good print housekeeping.

The main risk comes from the stencil-cleaning chemicals used in photo silkscreen, so make sure you have the right protective clothing. Always refer to the Government Health and Safety guidelines and identify what hazards are associated with each product you use by reading the safety sheets. (COSHH/Control of Substances Hazardous to Health. Published by the Government HSE (Health and Safety Executive) and available online.)

Decide who might be harmed too, as anyone can be at risk in a home studio environment. Look at how you can control the risks and prevent exposure. Consider how you might be able to change the process to reduce the risk.

Plan how you will store your materials and equipment. Ensure that everything is labelled correctly, has a properly fitting lid and that incompatible materials such as ink and cleaning products are kept separately.

Have the right materials at hand to clean up spillages quickly and safely.

Plan your storage and waste.

Always clean your hands after printing. A good citrus hand cleaner should be used, never a spirit or solvent.

ESSENTIAL PROTECTIVE CLOTHING

- Protective apron for use when printing. A plastic apron should always be used when cleaning screens with a power washer
- Disposable gloves, preferably chemical-resistant nitrile gloves, for when handling emulsion or cleaning screens
- Ear defenders for when using a power washer or cleaning screens with a hosepipe
- Respirator or face mask for use when using chemicals, spraying glue and so on
- Goggles to prevent the spray getting into your eyes when cleaning screens using a power washer

ENVIRONMENTAL CONSIDERATIONS

Every effort should be made to reduce your impact on the environment when silkscreen printing. I have a rigorous regime to reduce consumption of materials and recycle as much as possible.

Waste management system

Although the process we are going to use is water based, the inks are acrylic and rely on plastic resins or binders, pigments and various chemical additives.

All the ink should be removed from screens after printing with a plastic chisel-shaped palette knife. Keep all acrylic ink, regardless of the colour mix, in recycled pots with lids and wash the screens in a bowl of water with a microfibre cloth after the ink has been removed. Don't pour ink down the drain. After you have finished printing for the day, leave the water bowl with dirty water to one side. Overnight the acrylic particles settle to the bottom. The next day, carefully, and without disturbing the sediment, pour the almost clear water away, taking care to leave the sludge in the bottom of the bowl. Wipe the sludge up with a paper towel and bin it. You'll be amazed how much there is.

Reduce consumption and waste by using paper tapes. Decorators' tapes have excellent water resistance and can be washed without removal. Try to limit your use of plastic parcel tape, as it leaves a sticky deposit on screens that is difficult to remove and requires robust cleaning that can damage your screen.

Don't mix paper waste with inky tapes. Keep them separate: I have two waste bins in my studio for this purpose.

Recycled paper

Use recycled paper such as newsprint where possible, especially when you are starting out. Leave more expensive papers until you are more experienced. The price will curb your enthusiasm.

Upcycle

I upcycle all my waste printing products. They can be cut up to use in collage, sold as seconds or made into other products such as Christmas decorations and book covers. I always proof print on the backs of prints too.

PRINTING EQUIPMENT

Screens

This is the most important piece of equipment and consists of a wooden or aluminium frame that is tightly stretched with a polyester fabric. Screens are professionally re-stretched using a purpose-built machine that pulls the fabric taut like a drum. The mesh is then bonded to the frame. Attempting to stretch your own by hand is a waste of time and resources.

The silkscreen frame has mesh stretched on one side and this is referred to as the back of the screen. The interior of the screen is known as the well, as it holds the ink when printing. The screen is attached to the printing base 'well side' up, while the 'back' of the screen is in contact with the paper and holds a stencil.

Screens are vulnerable to damage and great care should be taken to protect them from sharp and abrasive objects. Good quality screens are the basis of good quality prints and should be well cared for. They can last for many years and are an expensive, but worthwhile, investment. Stack frames side by side with cardboard placed inbetween. Be very careful when moving screens around together as the corners of aluminium frames can easily puncture the underlying mesh.

As the printing system we are going to use is water-based and screens will get wet in the cleaning process, metal frames are recommended. Wooden screens are generally cheaper and require a waterproof varnish such as PVA glue. Several wooden frames that I have had re-stretched over the years are now starting to warp.

Screens are covered in a tightly woven mesh that allows ink to pass through. This is controlled by a thread count size, which is specified when you order: a 90-thread count is generally fine for most paper printing, rising to a 120 thread-count for capturing more detailed work associated with photo-silkscreen, such as fine lines and small typography. The thread number relates to the number of overlapping threads per inch: the lower the number the greater the ink flow through the mesh. Lower thread counts are used for printing onto textile, where a greater flow of ink is required.

I would recommend a 90 mesh when starting out as it is less likely to block with ink and is also easy to clean.

Screen dimensions are measured on external dimensions. I use a screen size of 48 × 60cm for A4 printing as this allows plenty of space to print around the image without damaging the edge of the screen.

Printing baseboard and hinges

The screen is attached to the print board and held in place using a couple of metal butterfly hinges that are attached permanently to the edge of the board. The hinges clamp onto the edge of the screen and enable it to move up and down during the printing process and be easily removed for cleaning after printing. The screw hinges stop the screen from moving during printing and have a gripping surface. Make sure that you get these as tight as possible during printing as any movement in the screen will cause problems with print registration and subsequent colours may not be aligned.

I recommend a baseboard that is cut larger than the screen and is washable. An old kitchen cupboard door with some rubber foot stops can easily be constructed and stored upright with the screen attached when not in use. Printing baseboards with the hinges inset into the base are also available commercially.

Alternatively, the hinges can be attached permanently to a flat solid table. This works well if you are going to use very large screens and have the space. Don't try this on the kitchen table though.

Printing equipment essentials.

Squeegee

This comprises a wooden or metal handle holding a rubber blade that can be replaced. There are different kinds of blades, however, of which a medium square cut is suitable for most work on paper. The blade edge deposits a thin coat of ink on the paper beneath the screen as it is pulled over.

For printing A4 a squeegee a couple of centimetres larger than the printing area, about 25cm, is required.

Ink

There are lots of acrylic water-based printing inks available to use. Some are premixed, while others are diluted with a silkscreen printing medium that decreases the viscosity of the ink and makes it easy to pull across the screen.

Silkscreen printing medium

I use a clear printing medium that is suitable for silkscreen printing onto paper and mix it into acrylic paint to create specific shades and colours. The printing medium is added to ink in different ratios depending on the opacity you require. Printing medium is often called printing binder.

When you are starting out I suggest using a 50:50 ratio. I use a 20:80 ratio for opaque colours and increase the ratio for paler shades by adding more binder.

Screen binder also stops the acrylic drying into the screen when you are printing. Although we will be using an acrylic printing system in this book, many printmakers experiment with eco dyes on both paper and textile.

Acrylic ink system

A wide range of colours are available to use that correspond to the colour wheel. When mixed or overlapped during the printing process, these provide an extensive range of shades, tones and tints.

Paint manufacturers have also created a four-colour system: cyan, magenta, process yellow and process black. This paint system corresponds to four-colour process printing and provides a good set of starter inks with the addition of Titanium white. Other specialised colours can be added including fluorescents and metallics.

When mixed with screen binder the ink should be the consistency of double cream. If the mix is overly thick you can add a few drops of water to thin it down. Equally if you have stored ink that has thickened over time the addition of water will bring it back into use.

Acrylic inks are light, fast and are safe to use. Make sure you store them with airtight lids as they can dry out when left uncovered. Choose acrylic ink with a good quality pigment that is easy to source.

A protective apron is always required during printing as ink cannot be removed when it has dried. Ink should be cleaned off the screen with warm clean water as soon as you have finished printing. Some colours including darker pigments, such as black and blue, can leave stains on the mesh if they are not removed properly, and this will degrade future print quality.

I keep all my removed inks as they are surprisingly useful when you need a specific neutral grey tone.

Retarder

Retarder can be added to the printing ink to slow down the drying time of screen-printing inks. It can prevent the screen from blocking up and makes it easier to clean. Retarder is particularly useful in hot weather. A few drops are added when you are mixing the ink.

Palette knives

Chisel-shaped plastic palette knives are used to remove excess ink from screens and ones with a straight design are preferred for mixing ink. They are cheap, long-lasting and easy to clean. I avoid using anything metal on my screens. Rubber domestic palette knives are banned from my studio as they are difficult to use efficiently and too big for my ink pots.

Plastic pots

Start collecting plastic pots with lids, if possible, to mix and store ink. Once mixed ink can be saved for a couple of months if tightly sealed. I keep mine out of sunlight and stacked in a box

PAPER

There are so many different roles for paper within the silkscreen printing process and it is important to consider how you are going to use and recycle them. Paper is an expensive commodity and should be treated with respect. Inevitably when you are starting out you will be eager to generate as many copies of a design as possible. I strongly suggest that you restrain your print editions when you start and set modest quantities.

Printing papers

A range of papers can be used for silkscreen printing. Since the process is water-based, however, very thin papers can 'cockle' or distort when large areas of ink are printed. Keeping paper in damp conditions can also cause cockling, so it should be kept in a dry, flat storage area.

Pre-cut paper saves time and reduces waste

Hand-cut paper stencils can easily be made using newsprint or freezer paper.

Flat hot-press paper is recommended. It has a smooth feel and can be sourced in any art shop. A sketching book of 250gsm cartridge paper can be removed from the paper block and kept ready to use. You can also buy pre-cut printing paper in larger quantities. Source 300gsm if possible. It is also more cost-effective to buy in quantity, say 100 sheets.

Proof-printing is best undertaken on newsprint or photocopy paper. Pre-cut greetings cards are also a great way to buy paper stock that is cut to size and ready to use. You can get lots of different colours, shapes and weights. Make sure that you use 250–300gsm card for greetings cards as anything less will fall when folded.

Brown paper rolls are great for repeat patterns for items such as wrapping paper.

Paper for hand-cut stencils

Freezer paper is a good choice for paper-stencil making that can be reused as it is easy to cut and remove from the screen after printing. it is also thin enough to create fine detail without blocking the screen. Newsprint and photocopy paper can also be used, but be careful as some photocopy paper can stick to the screen and be difficult to remove after printing. I regularly use newsprint for paper stencils but prefer magazine-quality paper as it has good resistance to ink and is very strong.

SCREEN FILLER AND DRAWING FLUID

Screen filler and drawing fluid are used to create a semi-permanent hand-painted screen stencil. The filler can be used on its own or in conjunction with the drawing fluid to make both positive and negative designs. A chemical is required to remove the stencil after you have finished printing.

The filler can also be used to fill small holes in photo stencils.

PHOTO SILKSCREEN

A detailed explanation of the photo silkscreen process will be provided in Chapter 5. Below is an overview of the equipment and materials you will need.

Exposure unit

My preferred method of exposing screens is by using a box to contain the UV light that is used in the process. The light is positioned in the bottom of the unit and a glass top holds the screen throughout the exposure. You can make a box or utilise any large container. How the system works will be explained in Chapter 5.

There are several alternative methods of screen exposure including suspending UV lights above the screen. Both methods work well and lots of information on how to set up the lights is available from suppliers.

Photo emulsion

Photo emulsion is a two-part chemical that is mixed and used to coat the screen. When it is dried it is sensitive to UV light. Mixed emulsion has a shelf life of approximately three months. If kept in the fridge this can be extended.

Emulsion coating trough

A metal trough that is used to apply emulsion to the back of the screen.

Artist Nikki Williams has repurposed a storage box on wheels as her exposure unit. See how it fits snuggly under her workbench alongside her printing board and four screens.

Emulsion de-coating solution

This is used to remove the stencil after printing and to reclaim the screen. You should always wear gloves and protect your eyes when using this.

DIGITAL PRINTING

You can use a home inkjet printer to output on acetate and make stencils for photo silkscreen. Film is readily available online and the only restriction is the size as most home printers are A4. You will need to experiment with the printing settings to achieve print opacity. Inkjet printers are also expensive to run, and I only use the black and white setting to keep the cost down.

For A3 positives I use a local copy shop where I keep a supply of acetate that is suitable for photocopier. It's worth noting that most copy shops don't tend to keep acetate in stock.

A makeshift washing line can be used to dry prints.

DRYING EQUIPMENT

As my space is limited I don't have a drying rack, but instead use a washing line strung across my studio. Small prints can also be dried on a table. If you wish, however, small drying racks are available and larger ones that hang from the ceiling.

GENERAL KIT

Pencils, rubbers etc.
A selection of soft drawing pencils for general use as well as some coloured pencils for design work.

Scissors and craft knives
Good quality scissors and sharp craft knives are essential for all kinds of jobs associated with printing. Keep them in a safe place and maintain their cutting edges. Care should be taken when working near screens.

Guillotine
For cutting paper I use a rotary blade guillotine. It is in use every day and I don't know how I would manage without it. It's easy to store against a wall too when not in use.

Spray glue
Used to keep prints in place on the printing baseboard during the print process. When applying this use a respirator or face mask.

Tapes
Essential for masking the well of screens prior to printing. There is a range of tapes available. I use a water-retarding decorators' masking tape for most jobs. Plastic parcel tape is good for masking screens for monoprinting and where a waterproof mask is required when using paper stencils. Screens can be washed after printing and the plastic tape can be left in place.

Cutting mat and metal ruler
General paper cutting, making hand-cut paper stencils and registration stops.

Light box
Not essential, but useful for designing and painting photo stencils and registering colours. LED slim-line light boxes are a great design innovation and energy efficient.

Paintbrushes
Keep a good selection of brushes both large and small for painting directly on the screen during the monoprinting process, making hand-painted stencils and similar uses.

Glue stick
Solid adhesive pushed from a tube to stick artwork into position. Can be used to collage transparent films.

CLEANING

If you let acrylic ink dry in the printing mesh you can say goodbye to your screen. That's why it so important to remove all residue ink as soon as you have finished printing. Most ink can be removed with warm water. I use a bucket of water to do this if I'm monoprinting. When you have finished, both sides of the screen can be hosed down with a garden hose.

Hose or power washer
A garden hose with a spray attachment is fine for most cleaning jobs and washing out photo stencils. When removing photo emulsion, however, a small power washer is preferable and will save you a lot of time.

Cloths and buckets
Microfibre household cleaning cloths should be used to clean screens and wash out tools at the end of the printing process. A bucket or washing-up bowl is always useful too.

Citrus-based cleaner
After working with Indian ink or degreasing screens the brushes can be cleaned in a citrus-based product such as Citri-Clean. This can also be used for removing dried acrylic ink on screens.

Access to an outside hosepipe can save you time cleaning your screens.

Pink Stuff
Difficult acrylic stains can be removed with a cleaning paste cleaner, such as Pink Stuff, which can be applied to the screen mesh. It is mildly abrasive, so use with care. Apply with a sponge or brush and remove with plenty of water.

Degreaser
Degreaser is applied to the screen after cleaning. It is generally used to make sure that any dust and grease is removed before applying photo emulsion. Degreaser is diluted with water, rubbed into the screen and then removed with a hose spray. The screen is left to dry before being coated.

MONOPRINTING DRAWING AND PAINTING MATERIALS

The techniques I use to create my monoprint silkscreens use water-based crayons, paint and graphite. They can be combined with acrylic paint and are easy to use and clean off the screen.

Graphite pencils
Soft (2B) stubby pencils are perfect for monoprinting, linear drawing and smudging. Stay away from anything softer as the graphite can be hard to remove from the screen.

Water-based wax drawing crayons
These are essential for the monoprinting process. Make sure you use the water-based and not the oil pastel variety or you will have difficulty removing the crayon from the screen.

Water-based paint
Any watercolour paint as well as gouache can also be used in the monoprinting process. Paint can be mixed and stored on palettes for reuse.

PHOTO STENCIL POSITIVES

An explanation of how to make hand-drawn/painted stencils or positives for photo silkscreen will be found in Chapter 5. The process involves drawing or painting a design onto a film using an opaque drawing or painting medium that can block out ultraviolet light during the exposure process.

The following materials provide an overview of what you can use to make handmade positives:

Films and drawing surfaces

Clear acetate sheets or florist film make ideal surfaces for painting or drawing with acrylic pens or Indian ink. You can also use more expensive films such as Maylar and Mark Resist or good-quality tracing paper. The different mark-making qualities you can achieve will be described in Chapter 5.

Painting and drawing

There is a large choice of drawing and painting materials that you can use to create handmade stencils. Avoid felt-tip pens as they are not opaque enough to resist UV light. Opt instead for acrylic pens such as those made by Posca, which come in a range of nib tips including brushes. These work well and you can achieve a range of marks. They are easy to scratch and add sgraffito marks too.

I use a good-quality Indian ink to hand-paint onto Maylar or other transparent material. Textured rubbings can be made from wallpaper, net/lace, thin plastic, sequin waste and so on using wax crayons.

SKETCHBOOKS AND CREATIVE INSPIRATION

One of the biggest barriers to silkscreen is developing your ideas into print. There are so many steps to making a print work both in terms of the process and your expectations. My work is quite experimental and I utilise lots of different techniques in my prints. Some methods such as paper cut-out stencils are very graphic, whereas monoprint may suit a more direct drawing style.

I use sketchbooks as a daily form of creative expression, and this is where my prints are developed. I suggest that you find a way of collecting ideas, perhaps in the form of a mood board or a digital/paper scrapbook.

You can experiment with a wide range of transparent films and drawing materials when creating stencils for photo silkscreen.

It is handy to keep sketchbooks and draw from life on a regular basis.

CHAPTER 2

GETTING STARTED WITH SILKSCREEN BASICS

Learning to screen-print for the first time in the home environment may seem like a challenge, yet when you pull your first print and excitedly lift the screen off the paper to reveal the finished design, the thrill to do it again is difficult to contain. It's so simple to push ink through a stencil and make a series of prints that it sets your imagination working on how you can utilise the process.

You might make some cards, create a poster or explore the technique further and decorate some fabric. Sharing most print activities with a friend or family member can also be a rewarding and fun experience and a chance to join forces and work together. Children and young people are always amazed by the simplicity of silkscreen and can easily participate with help in both the printing and stencil making.

In this chapter we will be making and using paper stencils to learn the mechanics of the silkscreen process. If you are a complete beginner I suggest you follow the step-by-step instructions before moving to the more advanced chapters. We will cover the basic print set-up, design, how to make simple stencils, ink mixing, registration and the use of printing equipment. All these skills need to be mastered to give you confidence in the equipment and materials and in your home set-up.

Design considerations are also covered in this chapter and it's a good idea to keep a sketchbook or idea/mood board to hand where you can gather inspiration when making stencils. A digital inspiration board is a good way of collating work that inspires as well as sharing your own individual progress. Just a small doodle, magazine cut-out or a series of simple drawings are useful to have available when you are at a loss for inspiration.

To test your skills, I have included a project at the end of the chapter that will help you explore simple multicoloured prints.

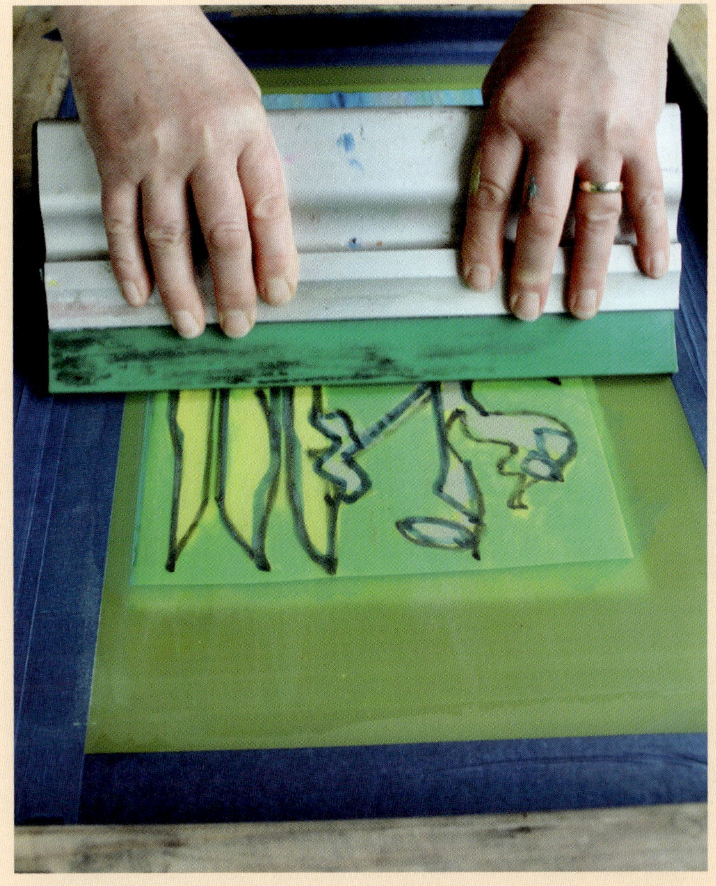

Printing equipment essentials

Simple paper stencils may be cut from freezer paper or newsprint.

OVERVIEW OF THE PRINTING PROCESS

This chapter is designed to get you started with print basics using simple hand-cut stencils as a way of printing a design through a silkscreen mesh onto paper that is positioned below the screen. It's a simple way of printing and relies on cutting or tearing designs into paper to create a stencil.

Stencils are positioned under the screen and are 'picked up' during the printing process sticking themselves to the underside of the mesh and blocking the screen. After printing they are removed and can be reused.

Preparing your stencils is a major component of the printing process and should be undertaken in advance of the printing session. In this chapter we will be making very simple stencils from paper and newsprint.

Designing your stencil will be the first part of the printing process. Here you will learn to make stencils that use bridges to keep all the cut elements together as well as experimenting with overlapping stencils using different coloured inks.

Only the most basic equipment is needed. Learning this method will underpin your understanding of the whole process and how it can be developed into very sophisticated prints.

Another important area of preparation is to mask off your screen to create a printing area that can be used for both paper stencil and monoprinting. Masked screens are an important resource and should be cleaned and reused.

You will discover that silkscreen is a quick printing process once you get started. However, ink can also dry very quickly on the screen, and you just can't walk away from your printing table to sort out where you are going to hang your prints and expect your screen mesh to stay in good printing condition when you get back. Inks dry into the printing mesh extremely quickly and if you are not prepared for this the whole experience can be very frustrating.

I encourage you to stick with the process and experiment with lots of different stencil cut-outs, some of which you can discard but others you may be able to use again. I also make stencils from thin film as they are more robust than paper, so can be cleaned, stored and reused.

Multicoloured paper-stencil print using free-floating, hand-cut stencils that are printed, removed and replaced in different positions to create a multilayered print.

SETTING UP YOUR WORKSPACE

Organisation is the key with any printing process. All equipment and materials need to be at hand along with thoughts about all the printing issues that you may encounter. Always consider the space where you are going to make your screen prints. Do you have access to a sink and water? Where will you dry your prints, and which surface will you utilise to set up your printing kit? Do you have a damp cloth? Are the palette knives at hand and where is the masking tape?

You may need to consider other people or animals who are sharing your space. Over-enthusiastic dogs and children can easily topple your printing ink on the floor and walk it into your new fitted carpet. A space where you can operate on your own without interruption is essential when you start to print, so bear this in mind when you try it out for the first time. Kitchens are a great place to start, although you should keep in mind that acrylic paint will stick to surfaces and floors if left to dry.

Wash out area

Access to a sink and water is a major consideration for cleaning screens at the end of a printing session. The recommended screen size will fit in most kitchen sinks for cleaning. It is even better If you have access to a garden power washer or hosepipe and outside drain. Use microfibre cleaning cloths to clean screens as they are easy to wash and reuse.

Clean workspace

Designing and preparing artwork is an essential part of the process and is generally undertaken separately from the printing area. I suggest that you set aside a clean drawing and cutting space where you can work on designs, store your materials and generally concentrate on your creativity.

Storage and waste

Setting up equipment is one thing but you should also consider the clearing away and storage. This will keep you focused on getting the most out of the process and less frustrated about where you put the squeegee last time you used it. Consider where you will put your printing waste too. Most of the printing stencils and removable screen tapes we will be using can be recycled and I suggest that you keep all prints for future test prints or collage.

My clean workspace is tightly packed with drawing and stencil-making equipment and materials.

EQUIPMENT AND MATERIALS

The equipment I have suggested for a print beginner can be stored together in a box, apart from the screen and the baseboard, which can be leant upright against a wall in a garage or shed when not in use, or if you are tight for space, placed flat under a bed. The screen can be stored attached to the hinged brackets and a piece of cardboard attached to protect the mesh from any sharp objects when not in use. Small screens can be stacked on a shelf, either on top of one another or side by side.

The screen is attached to the baseboard with the hinge clamps. Find a good printing position so that that you do not have to stretch too far over the screen.

Screen and baseboard

Screens and baseboards are your printing essentials. The silkscreen frame is fitted into the hinge carriers at the top of the printing baseboard and screwed tight. Place the baseboard on a flat surface that will be your printing table, making sure it is waist height. It's important that you are in a good printing position for your height, that you can reach over the screen and apply pressure without too much stretching.

The hinges will keep the screen in the same position for every print but can easily be unscrewed after printing. The screen can be moved up and down into print position. A used roll of masking tape can hold the screen in a slightly elevated position between printing.

You will need space on either side of the table to accommodate printing paper, the inky squeegee between prints and any other materials that you might need, such as a palette knife, masking tape and a wet cloth.

BASIC PRINTING KIT

To get started you will require the following or similar-sized equipment and materials that will be suitable for printing A4:

* Silkscreen baseboard with hinge clamps (78 × 54cm)
* Screen (90 mesh) with internal measurements approx. 48 × 60cm
* Squeegee (28cm)
* Bucket of water and cleaning cloth
* Paper
* Plastic tape
* Stencil paper
* Craft knife and cutting board
* Ink and screen binder
* Palette knives

CREATING A PRINTING MASK

Before attaching the screen to the baseboard for printing you will first need to make a basic printing mask to create a printable area. This will be essential for the paper pickup stencils you are going to use or any future monoprinting.

There are three methods of making a printing mask:

* Using plastic tape, overlaid in the well of the screen and masked to the edge of the frame. This is the method described below
* Masking the screen with screen filler
* Using a photo stencil to create a masked area (see Chapter 5)

Method

A printing mask is an open area of the screen that acts as the printing area. It is created by taping off unwanted mesh with a waterproof plastic tape that extends to the edge of the printing mesh.

As we will be printing onto A4 paper, we are going to make a mask that is slightly smaller, providing a 2cm border around our printed area. This will allow room to handle the print on the edges. The mask stops the ink from bleeding into unwanted areas and protects the screen. It's a simple way to get started. When you have more experience, however, you may consider keeping a photo stencil mask on a screen permanently to use in this process as it's more hard-wearing and prevents ink from bleeding under the tape and onto the paper edge. Instructions on how to make this are given in Chapter 5.

EQUIPMENT AND MATERIALS

* Screen
* Plastic parcel tape – any colour will do
* Small pieces of cardboard approx. 4 × 4cm
* Soft pencil (2B)
* A4 paper
* Ruler
* Scissors

Masked screens should be thoroughly cleaned at the end of a printing session on both sides with warm water before drying and storing, taking care not to damage the mask edges.

Draw the mask on the screen

Lay the screen on the printing table well side up. Place a piece of A4 paper in the centre, allowing a gap of about 10cm at the top and 13cm at the bottom. Use a soft pencil to draw the paper outline onto the screen. Be careful not to press too hard. Remove the paper. The reason for the extra space at the bottom is to give you extra space when you print.

Masking the screen

Use plastic parcel tape in the well of the screen and firmly mask off the external areas around the drawn outline, cutting the tape with scissors prior to application. Always take care that sharp objects are kept away from the screen. Mask off the screen sides with paper masking tape. This will protect the screen frame and stop the ink from getting under the screen.

Draw around a sheet of paper slightly smaller than A4 placed in the middle of the screen.

Using plastic tape, mask the perimeter of the drawn shape on the screen.

Continue masking by overlapping the tape right onto the edges of the frame.

MAKING PAPER STENCILS

Silkscreen is a stencil-based process, and we are going to create our own simple hand-cut stencils from paper. The next chapter will cover this process in more detail, but to get started we will practise using this basic method.

Method

Simple clear designs are required. These are either cut or torn out of thin paper, which can resist the water-based ink and be discarded or reused. Stencils are attached to the underside of the screen and are picked up during the printing process: stencils do not need to be taped in position.

Stencil paper preparation

Paper stencils can be created from various types of paper. Paper that resists ink is best, such as freezer paper, newsprint and greaseproof paper. Some photocopier paper can stick to the screen, making it difficult to remove the stencil, so I tend not to use it.

Whatever paper you use, cut the paper to A4 size and draw a 2cm border around the edge with a pencil. Your design will fit within the border. It's important that your stencils fit within the printing area and there is an overlap with the screen-printing mask. The border creates an overlap and ensures that the ink does not bleed through the edges of the design when printed.

Design considerations

Consider your design carefully, bearing in mind that the areas you remove in the stencil and cut away will print; areas that are left behind in the paper will remain the colour of the printing paper.

EQUIPMENT AND MATERIALS

* Masking tape
* A4 paper – sketchbook paper can be removed from the spine
* A4 photocopier paper, silicone stencil paper or newsprint/thin paper
* Cutting board and metal ruler
* Craft knife or scalpel and scissors
* Pencil
* Black pen
* Design inspiration

A 2cm border marks out the space in which the design must fit.

Try playing with coloured paper silhouettes to create a design.

After the design has been created within the intended space, use a black pen to outline the shapes that you are going to remove.

Remove the design with a sharp craft knife. Keep your other hand away from the direction of the cut.

Place the cut stencil on a coloured piece of card to preview how it will print. Alternatively, you can use scissors to cut out simple shapes, paper strips or patterns. When creating your stencil, you may need to build in paper bridges that connect areas of the design and keep the stencil together.

If you have difficulty using a craft knife, use a sharp pair of scissors and fold the stencil paper before cutting to reveal symmetrical shapes.

Draw the design on stencil paper

Aim to create a design that covers the paper, but doesn't stray into the border area as this is where the paper will cover the screen mask. Consider which areas you want to print and which areas will remain the white of the paper background. Thin strips can be difficult to print using this method, so keep the design bold and uncomplicated.

Stencil cutting

Using a craft knife and cutting board, cut out the stencil, ensuring that it stays in one piece. When it's complete put it aside.

I keep the cut shapes from stencils and use them in overlays.

REGISTERING PAPER STENCILS

To ensure that your prints land in the same place on the printing paper you need to add registration stops to the baseboard underneath the screen. This will ensure alignment during the printing process. Registration is a key part of the printing process as it ensures that your print is always properly aligned on the paper. When subsequent colours are applied on top they also line up with the under-colours.

EQUIPMENT AND MATERIALS

* Masked screen and baseboard (attached)
* Cutting board
* 5cm masking tape
* Thick cardboard strips (3 × 3cm)
* Soft pencil
* Craft knife
* Scissors
* Printing paper
* Ruler
* Spray glue
* Newsprint

Making registration stops
Position four layers of masking tape on top of each other on a cutting board. Make a clean cut on one edge using a metal ruler and remove the excess tape. Cut three squares of tape and leave attached to the board. Alternatively, cut three pieces of thick card (3 × 3cm), ensuring that the edges are straight. These are the registration stops.

Aligning 'master print' paper with screen
Draw a rectangle with a 2cm border on A4 printing paper. This is the 'master print' that mirrors the screen mask. Place it under the screen and align the pencil border with the mask. This can be a tricky procedure, but it is important to ensure that they line up exactly. Lightly tape the 'master print' to the baseboard.

Applying three registration stops
Remove three of the registration stops from the cutting board. Accurately butt up to the bottom left-hand corner of the 'master print' at right angles. Place a further mark about three quarters of the way along the bottom edge. If using the card method, tape the pieces in position.

Method

Mis-registration is a common problem, so patience and careful paper positioning are crucial for best results. In this section we will learn how to use tape/card registration stops for a one-colour print. Each piece of printing paper slides easily into these registration slots and out after each print is removed, making way for the next piece.

Add spray glue to the baseboard

During the printing process it is important that the paper stays attached to the baseboard, so it is worth applying a fine layer of spray glue to the printable area on the baseboard. Mask off the print area with newspaper, remove the printing paper and spray the area very lightly. This should be done outside and wearing a mask.

Preparing stencil pickup

Fit the printing paper into the registration stops on the baseboard under the screen. Place the cut stencil on the paper and align with the drawn border. You are now ready to print.

Mix neat acrylic ink in equal parts (50:50) with printing binder.

Yellow-green, green, blue-green printing combination.

MIXING PRINTING INK

Before you start to print, consider what inks you are going to use, how you are going to mix them to achieve the right colours, and then store them in a way that is both cost-effective and reusable. Water-based silkscreen printing has transformed the process and made it much more accessible and easier to clean and reuse screens. Gone are the nasty oil-based inks and chemicals of the past, along with associated health problems and the impact on the environment.

Ink and printing binder

Inks are supplied premixed with a printing binder, or you can buy your own acrylic colours and mix them with a silkscreen binder. The screen binder is clear and has the consistency of single cream. Inks can be mixed and stored for up to three months if the containers have good lids. Don't be tempted to throw colour away as you will find that even a sludge brown can be used effectively. I recycle old margarine tubs and other food containers that have lids.

Never apply neat acrylic paint directly to a screen as it will stain and dry into the screen.

Mixing ink

Mixing water-based ink for print requires skill and is dependent on the quality of the pigments in your acrylic paint and how much binder you use to create a printing ink. Acrylic paint also comes in a range of different hues from warm to cool. Lemon yellow, for example, is a cool hue whereas cadmium yellow is warm. When you are just getting started, I would suggest a palette of basic primaries alongside black and white. As you become more confident you can add warm or cool colours to your ink collection.

The colour in the pot does not generally determine the printing colour as such a fine film is laid down in the printing process. I would suggest that you test the ink on the printing paper and maintain a scientific approach to applying binder.

Add equal parts of binder to pure colour (50:50) to get a good 'saturated' printing consistency. To achieve tonal values of the pure colour, add more binder. Binder can be accurately added by weight or volume.

All printing ink can be mixed to create a wide range of colour hues and saturation, and the addition of Titanium

White will both increase the opacity of the ink and give a lovely chalky appearance. Adding black can have very different effects: adding it to blue or red, for example, will give darker shades, but if you mix it with yellow you may get a range of greyish greens.

Colour combinations

Colour choice and application is as important as the design. The most basic colours, red, blue and yellow, are called primaries and cannot be created by mixing any other colours.

Secondary colours are created when two primaries are mixed together to produce a secondary colour: purple, orange or green.

Complementary colours are opposite one another on the colour circle and have the ability to complement and enhance one another. If you are looking to attract attention these colour combinations work well together:

* red and green
* yellow and purple
* blue and orange

To fill the colour circle, mix each adjacent primary-secondary colour pair to get a colour that is inbetween. These adjacent tertiary colours are a good choice to use together in a design because they harmonise with one another. Each colour has a tint of the other colour. For example:

* yellow-green, green, blue-green
* purple, red-purple and red
* orange, yellow-orange and yellow

Colour testing

When starting to mix your own inks I would suggest using an acrylic colour paint system including black, white, blue, yellow and red, together with a good silkscreen printing binder that is suitable for paper. Adding binder to acrylic paint will increase its transparency and once applied through a screen it will become even more translucent.

PRINTING TIPS

Using several printed layers of ink will increase the colour tone.

Ink is mixed to the consistency of runny cream; a small amount of water can also be added to help consistency. Ink can dry very quickly in hot weather, particularly during the printing process, so a dash of retarder can be added to reduce the drying time and give you more flexibility with your printing.

Experimenting with colour mixing is a very important part of the printing process. As you progress you will understand how transparent inks change when overprinted and how opaque colours can be used to block out or enhance shapes. You can test printing inks before printing by rubbing a small dot into an offcut of printing paper or, better still, printing a small area through a screen.

Printing on coloured paper

The colour of the paper will also determine the final print outcome. If you print on kraft paper, for example, which has a brownish tint, most primary colours will take on a greyish tint.

Scrape a small dot of printing ink across the paper with a flat palette knife to check the density of the printing ink.

HAND-PRINTING

Once all the pre-print organisation has been done, printing can get underway. Hand-printing using a squeegee is all about pushing and pulling ink across the screen to make the print, before lifting the screen to remove and replace the paper. The ink may need to be replenished and the activity can be quite physical if you are undertaking it on your own. Getting someone to help when you are learning is a good idea as a helper can handle the paper supply and hang prints to dry, while you attend to the printing process.

It is important that there is a gap between the screen and the print baseboard. The mesh needs to lift off the paper during the printing process and snap back into position. To enable this the screen requires a slight lift at the front of the frame. I attach a couple of pieces of thick card on either side of the front of the screen. Make sure that they are the same width and attached with tape.

Method

Make sure that all your materials and equipment are ready: ink mixed, paper cut to size and stacked nearby, extra spray glue, palette knives and damp cloths and a water source such as a bucket. A line and pegs are more than adequate for drying prints or, if you are working small, a tabletop or counter will do to lay them out.

Place the masked screen and baseboard in the printing area. Make sure the registration marks are in place, the printing paper is fitted and the paper stencil is on top.

The printing process works by flooding the screen and stencil with ink using the squeegee, in a one-handed procedure. The flooding fills the open areas of the screen/stencil with a very fine layer of ink.

For initial practise printing I suggest that you mix one colour of your choice. Place it in a container with a lid so it can be reused.

Flooding the screen

First apply a thin layer of ink, the width of the squeegee, at the bottom of the screen. Hold the squeegee in your dominant hand and lift the screen up off the baseboard with the other. Angle the squeegee to 45 degrees and push the ink away from you across the masked area and about 10cm beyond the mask. Maintain contact with the screen and pull the squeegee towards your body about 5cm, leaving the ink in a neat line. Lift the squeegee and place it behind the ink line.

Print

After flooding, lower the screen to print. Using both hands on the squeegee, pull the ink towards you, applying firm pressure. This action deposits the flooded ink on the paper underneath the screen and picks up the paper stencil in the process.

Paper pickup stencils are an excellent introduction to the process and are literally lifted off the baseboard onto the underside of the screen during the first printing pull. Stencils remain stuck to the screen during printing and are removed at the end.

The stencil is now empty of ink and the flooding is repeated prior to each print. As the squeegee moves across the screen during printing it is only the sharp edge of the blade that contacts the paper and baseboard. As you pull it towards your body the screen will lift off the print during the process. The lift off is important as it stops the print smudging beneath.

Print drying times

Print drying times can vary and the water-based printing method is generally very quick. The addition of higher quantities of print binder generally results in a longer drying time, as would two layers of ink applied on top of one another in two pulls. You should generally leave between 30 minutes and an hour before applying subsequent layers, and three hours before removing it from the printing line. Check that prints are dry with the back of your hand.

Fitting paper and introducing a paper stencil
Lift the screen and let it stand up in the hinges. Place the printing paper on the baseboard and slide into the registration stops. Place the paper stencil on top and match up with the printing paper. Carefully lower the screen.

Applying ink and flooding the screen
Flooding fills the open areas of the screen/stencil with a very fine layer of ink. Add a long, even layer of ink at the bottom of the screen and keep it lifted off the baseboard with one hand. With the other hand, angle the squeegee at 45 degrees and push the ink away from you across the screen.

Printing
Place the screen down on the table and, using both hands, grip the squeegee at 45 degrees and apply enough downward pressure to feel the table underneath the screen. You should be able to feel the edge of the printing blade as you pull the squeegee and ink towards you across the screen and over the stencil area.

Stencil pickup and reflood
This first flood and print will result in the stencil attaching to the underside of the screen and is commonly referred to as the 'paper pickup' stencil. You have now created your first print, which should be removed from the baseboard and placed on the drying line. Flood the screen again ready for the next print in order to stop the screen drying out.

Preparing for the next print
After flooding, place the screen in the upright position. Lay the squeegee to one side on a used roll of tape so that you now have both hands free. Remove the print and hang it up. Make sure your hands are clean and then place the next sheet into position and repeat the process. You may need to add more ink if you are creating a large edition.

Colour mixing on the screen
To add other colours to your print you can experiment by applying ink to the top of the screen in the stencil areas. Use a long palette knife to apply small amounts of contrasting ink in a swift motion prior to flooding the screen. Flood the screen after the application then print. This will inevitably change the colour of the printing ink, so use it sparingly.

CLEANING THE SCREEN AND SQUEEGEE

Cleaning can be a messy job, so make sure you have everything at hand. Place some old newsprint under the screen and lay it down on top. There is no need to remove it from the baseboard as you can clean the screen in situ.

Remove all the excess ink from the squeegee with a square palette knife and put it in the ink pot. Clean the blade and handle with a damp, but not too wet, cloth. Avoid soaking as the squeegee may retain water in the handle.

Store all ink in pots with lids, marked with a colour spot for later identification.

Using the square palette knife, carefully remove all ink from the screen. It should be easy to scrape off the plastic tape. Make sure all the screen edges are cleaned too.

Remove the paper stencil and wash away any remaining ink using clean warm water, if possible, on both sides of the screen. Any ink particles left in the mesh will dry into the screen, blocking it for future use and making it very difficult to reclaim. If you are going to use the screen again, it can be hand-dried with a towel on both sides and you can also use the same registration stops.

If you have finished printing the screen can be cleaned in a sink. Be careful if using a wooden screen as too much wetting will warp the frame. Remove all tapes and registration stops from the baseboard and wash down all the tabletops. Store all equipment in the printing box. All paper used in cleaning should be appropriately recycled.

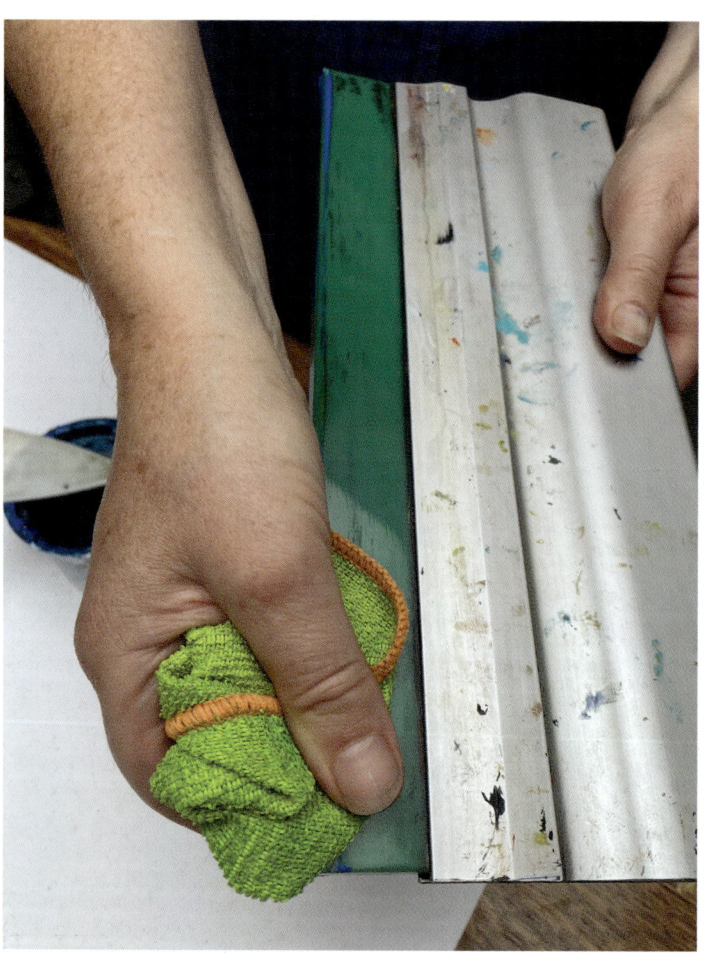

Remove ink from the squeegee.

Remove all ink from the screen with warm water and a microfibre cloth

TROUBLESHOOTING – PRINT

Uneven printing

Uneven printing is caused by a few printing difficulties, pressure being the main one. Check that you are holding the squeegee evenly and that you are not over-stretching. Good downward pressure is essential.

Too much snap can also make the printing pull very strenuous, so you may need to remove some of the card at the front of the screen (see Chapter 5).

You may find that some of your cut stencil areas are not printing, perhaps if you are attempting to cut some very thin lines or a tight corner. Make sure your paper stencils have rounded cuts and bold shapes and that you use a sharp craft knife. You may need to increase the downward pressure and pull the squeegee a second or third time to clear the stencil, making sure you do this without reflooding.

Cutting your stencils from thin paper is also important as thick paper can be difficult to get adherence to the screen and cause printing issues. I suggest that you use paper that is no thicker than 125gsm for paper pickup stencils.

Bleeding

Bleeding occurs where ink seeps under the stencil and appears on the paper where you don't want it. If bleeding is visible on the print, try keeping the squeegee at 45 degrees. If you use the blade vertically it can force too much ink through the mesh during the printing process. Bleeding can also occur if the ink is too thin, or the stencil has broken down and ink has got trapped underneath.

To clear a printing bleed, keep on printing on wastepaper or newsprint until the excess ink has run dry. The bleed is on the underside of the screen and will soon print away.

Blocked screen

Areas of the screen may have dried out and blocked with ink. This is one of the biggest screen-printing headaches and can be due to several reasons. If you are prepared for this in advance you should be able to carry out a quick remedy. Likely reasons are that ink has dried into the screen or there may not be enough ink on the screen, resulting in uneven flooding. The latter can easily be rectified by adding more ink to the printing area. For dried-in ink you may need to stop printing, remove the stencil and clean the screen before recommencing printing.

The speed at which you are printing can also result in blocked screens. You need to keep an even print speed to avoid this and make sure the stencil remains flooded between prints. If the ink starts to thicken and gets a sticky texture you may need to add a retarder to keep it open on the screen. This should be done in advance and when the printing environment is warm.

Print blotching and smudging

Make sure that the snap keeps the mesh and paper apart when you print. If it is too close the print will touch and cause blotching.

Uneven printing.

Bleeding.

PROJECT: COLOUR PAPER-STENCIL OVERLAYS

Now that you have undertaken your first one-colour print and have experience of the silkscreen printing process and how the equipment works, it is time to move on to colour overlays using more than one colour.

The following project is a simple task that will enable you to work with three transparent primary colours and look at how they respond to one another when overlaid in different configurations. You may want to expand this project by reducing the ink/binder ratios or adding black/white to the palette. Although the project works with the three primary colours, you don't have to stick with these, and you should feel free to experiment as much as possible.

By undertaking this project using different stencil shapes and ink ratios you will develop a collection of colour swatches that you can refer to when creating a print colour palette. Make sure that you note ink ratios and colours on the back of the print.

EQUIPMENT AND MATERIALS

* Masked screen
* Printing board
* Squeegee
* Palette knives
* Drying line and pegs
* Three primary acrylic inks
* Screen printing medium
* Inkpots
* A4 printing paper
* Newspaper
* Water bowl and cleaning cloths
* Masking tape
* Pencil

Multicoloured paper-stencil print.

Method

For this project use the same screen mask and register your A4 paper as before. Make your stencils out of newspaper, cutting random shapes with scissors or by hand. Place your stencils on the master page, flood the screen and pickup. Print the lightest colour first and repeat the steps by removing the stencils and cleaning and drying the screen before resuming the next stencil and colour. Make sure that you leave plenty of time between colours to ensure prints and mesh are dry.

It is worth noting that if you remove the paper stencils carefully at the end of the printing process and let them dry, they can be sprayed black and used in the photo-silkscreen process in Chapters 5 and 6.

Mix the inks
Mix up 50% ink and 50% print binder in the following colours – red, yellow and blue – and label all the pots.

Cut and tear the paper-stencil shapes and register printing paper
If you use printed newspaper, this will create a textured and soft printed edge. Use the A4 master copy to register and maintain the 2cm border. Apply registration stops to the baseboard.

Print yellow
Flood your screen with the first colour, yellow, and pick up the stencil shapes and print.

Remove the print and insert the next piece of paper
Continue to print your edition and remove the prints to the drying line.

Remove yellow paper stencils and clean screen
Remove all the yellow stencils after printing. Make sure to clean and dry the screen prior to next colour.

Place a yellow print in the registration stops and arrange the next set of stencils (red) on top. Position the shapes so that the colours overlap and print.

Dry the prints carefully, if possible overnight. Ensure that you leave them for at least an hour as the ink layering will make the paper quite wet and the prints may stick to the screen.

Arrange the final blue paper stencils on the print.

Print the blue stencils.

Remove the paper stencils, clean the screen and dry the prints.

CHAPTER 3

HANDMADE STENCILS

In this chapter we will continue our printing and design journey with further exploration into the handmade stencil process. Once again these are easy and accessible printing methods, but organisation remains the key to success. By this time, you should be confident with your home print setup and capable of using simple paper stencils to print small editions. You should be familiar with the printing problems that you may encounter and what works for you in your printing area.

My first silkscreen printing encounter took place when I was a teenager at school, I was fascinated by how easy it was to make bold abstract designs and repeat patterns by cutting up newspapers. Remarkably I have continued to use this exact method to create background colours as well as abstract monoprints.

Although paper is commonly used in basic stencil-making, you can use all kinds of thin materials that can block the screen and print a silhouette. Garden plants can also be used along with cellophane, paper stickers, sticky back plastic, sequin waste and so on. If it can lie flat and hasn't got any sharp edges or spikes, you can give it a go.

In this chapter we are also going to turn our attention to liquid fillers and blocking fluids that can be applied to the screen to create lines and painterly marks. This will enable you to move away from the paper cut-out effect and make stencils that print textured lines and features. As soon as you move on to the use of fillers in silkscreen printing you are beginning to get into new screen-cleaning territory, and you will require a specific stencil remover and access to warm water.

There isn't a right or wrong way to approach these printing methods, and they can be enthusiastically combined in one print.

Paper and filler stencils combined in one print.

Paper-stencil print.

A washing line of simple papercut stencil prints.

Simple designs work well with the paper-stencil technique.

OVERVIEW

All of the methods described in this chapter can be used extensively in the silkscreen printing process. Alongside the hand-painted monoprinting techniques covered in Chapter 4, you may decide to leave the photo silkscreen process well alone and find plenty to occupy your creativity in these methods. Cutting stencils from paper is an art. It requires practise and skill to master the craft knife and cut a clean, sharp line without tearing the stencil paper. Equally a torn paper edge can produce beautiful soft prints.

I have a bit of a love-hate relationship with screen filler because of its thickness and permanent nature when applied to the screen. These attributes when mastered, however, can have many advantages, especially when screen filler is used in conjunction with drawing fluid or reduction printing. Both methods require practise but they enable you to create marks and lines without using photo stencils.

In the course of this chapter we will cover the following topics:

* Multicoloured prints using paper stencils
* Free-floating newspaper stencils
* Creating stencils and textures with other materials
* Filler stencil making and printing
* Filler and drawing fluid stencils
* Reduction filler stencils and printing

Each process has a specific list of materials and equipment detailed at the start of the technique.

MULTICOLOURED PRINTS USING PAPER STENCILS

You have already started working with paper to block out the screen and you are now familiar with cutting a paper stencil with a craft knife or a pair of scissors.

The aim of this project is to create a four-colour A4 print in which one of the colours includes the paper. The colours will not overlap, and you should break down the component colour parts including the paper to create the design. Remember you are cutting paper stencils, so

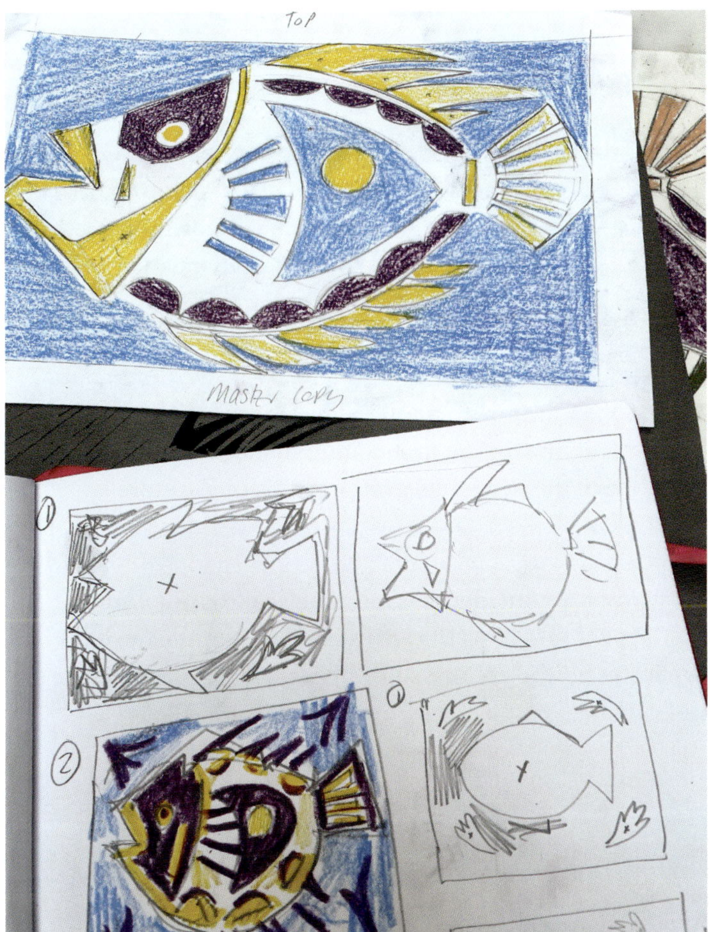

Thumbnail sketches are a great way of working out stencil design, structure and colour.

your design needs to be very simple. Your design should fit within the paper border of the master copy and each stencil should use paper bridges to ensure that each stencil stays intact.

Method

To make a multicoloured print using three colours you will require a design the same size as your A4 print. The design should allow for a 2cm border. Work your design up into a coloured sketch indicating the different coloured printing layers. Print the lightest colour first and apply further colours on top. I suggest that you start with a simple motif that fills the design space. Take your time over this and make some initial thumbnail drawings to develop your ideas. Try to ensure that your design fills the stencil area.

EQUIPMENT AND MATERIALS

* Clean screen (masked as demonstrated in Chapter 2)
* Squeegee
* Bucket of water and cleaning cloths
* Light box (optional)
* Printing paper
* A4 paper 'master copy'
* Stencil paper: freezer paper, newsprint, photocopier paper
* Cutting/craft knife
* Cutting board
* Squeegee
* Ink (three colours) and printing medium
* Masking tape
* Soft pencil
* Black felt-tip pen (permanent)
* Palette knives (wedge and thin)
* Apron and rubber gloves

Note: The master copy is a piece of A4 paper with a 2cm border; the paper border aligns with the edges of the screen mask.

Make sure that you utilise the paper colour and make it part of the design. The sketch should be accurate, and the colour scheme indicated on the sketch.

Outline the completed design with a black pen. This will enable you to trace through your design onto the stencil paper.

The print will fit within the masked area and have a 2cm border. Each paper stencil can be removed after printing and the screen cleaned in situ before printing the further colours. Leave time between printing each colour and don't remove the screen or registration stops in between printing.

Copy the design onto stencil paper

Tape your completed colour design to a flat surface. This is where a light box can help with the process of tracing the design onto the stencil paper.

You will need three sheets of stencil paper each with a 2cm border drawn in from the edge. Start by labelling the sheet with the appropriate printing colours. Place each stencil sheet on top of the design and outline each colour using a pencil to mark the areas that will be cut away. Indicate the top and bottom on each stencil.

FREEZER PAPER

Note that this has two sides: matte and shiny. Trace your design on the shiny side, which is the side that will be attached to the screen. Freezer paper comes on a roll, so it should be cut and flattened in advance of cutting the stencils.

Cut stencils

Transfer the outlined stencils to a cutting board and tape securely. Use a sharp craft knife to cut away the design. Make sure that each stencil stays intact and consider allowing for any bridges that need to be made to hold the design together. Stencil bridges are connections within a design that prevent it from falling apart and keep its structure.

Each stencil when placed on top of the other should line up to create the whole design. If they are placed on a light box, you will be able to see how the design fits together.

Put your cut stencils somewhere safe until you need them.

Test colours

Test the colour scheme on a clean piece of printing paper before printing and mix all the colours in advance. This can be done with a squeegee and some wastepaper. Let colours dry in between and label the ink containers.

Registering the print

Place an A4 master copy on the baseboard with a pencil border and line up the first colour stencil with the master copy. Place the three registration stops in position.

Printing

It's generally considered good practice to print your lightest colours first. In this case, however, the design separates all the colours and there is no overlap, so it's not crucial.

Use a sharp scalpel and cutting board to cut away the design.

Test your colour choice by taping off an area of the masked screen and apply ink using a small squeegee or piece of card.

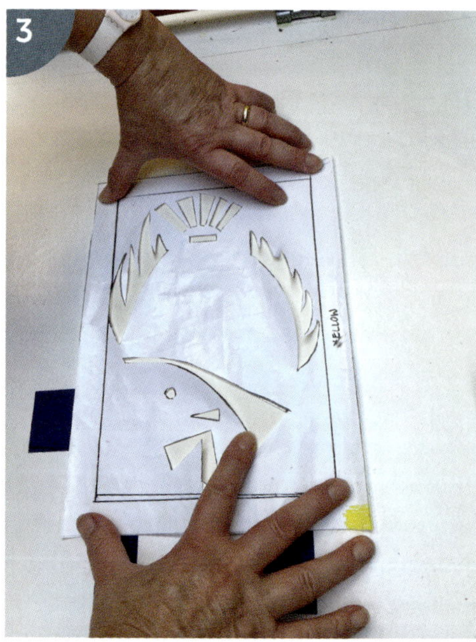

Line up the master copy with the screen printing area. Add three registration stops. Align the first stencil with the master copy.

Lift the screen and apply ink in a line at the bottom of the screen. Flood the screen mask with the first colour and lower the screen. Pull the squeegee across the masked area to print. The paper stencil will pick up and attach itself to the underside of the screen and cover the masked area. Paper stencils pick up easily on the screen and don't generally need taping.

The first print will land on the master copy, and you can see if it has printed within the border. Minor adjustments to the registration can be made at this point. The master copy will be the first copy for all the subsequent colours. If you are happy with the registration, continue printing the edition and hang the prints to dry. The master copy will help you to make any print adjustments and is the first test print.

After printing, carefully remove the stencil from the screen, lifting it from the top of the screen, and laying it inky side up on a piece of newsprint. When dry you can use it again. Keep it flat.

Leave the prints to dry for 20 minutes before collecting them together and moving on to the next colour. Remove all the ink from the squeegee and screen. Wash the screen and make sure it is completely dry before printing the next colour.

Place a dry copy of the first print into the registration stops and align the second stencil on top of where you want to print. Print the second colour. The second colour should fit around the first without any overlaps and start to define the design.

The final stencil is aligned with the master copy and printed to reveal the final design. A splash of extra colour was added to some of the prints by layering some pale turquoise on the top of the screen before flooding with the top colour.

FREE-FLOATING NEWSPAPER STENCILS

An alternative way of working with paper stencils is to design a motif and cut it from the stencil paper, keeping both the stencil and the cut away piece. You can then use both as print motifs. This will result in a positive and negative of the motif. There is no need to work up a colour design as this method is experimental and you can make ad hoc decisions as the print develops.

You can continue to use the same stencils for the second colour but move them around the print, which will create an interesting overlapping design. This method uses free-floating stencils, so there is no need to create bridges.

Aim for three layers of colour that will overlap and work well together. Mix three colours, starting with a light shade, and move through the colour layers. You can mix colours on the screen too.

The same materials and equipment will be used as in the previous project, with the addition of three acrylic paint colours of your choice mixed with an equal quantity of print binder (50:50).

Method

Working within the A4 size, create several simple motifs and abstract shapes that fit within the masked screen area. It doesn't matter if they overlap the border. The aim is to print three layers and you can reuse the stencils. You will need to let each layer dry between printing.

Place the master copy on the printing base and register in the usual way. Arrange the stencils across the page. Print the first colour and remove the stencils. Leave the prints to dry before resuming with the second colour. Make sure that you leave the stencils ink side up.

When the print has dried, arrange the second layer of stencils on the print. Notice how you can block out colours underneath. Print the second layer, mixing colours on the screen to create new shades and expressive marks.

Repeat the process with the third layer.

Free-floating stencils can be lifted off and replaced on the screen throughout the printing process.

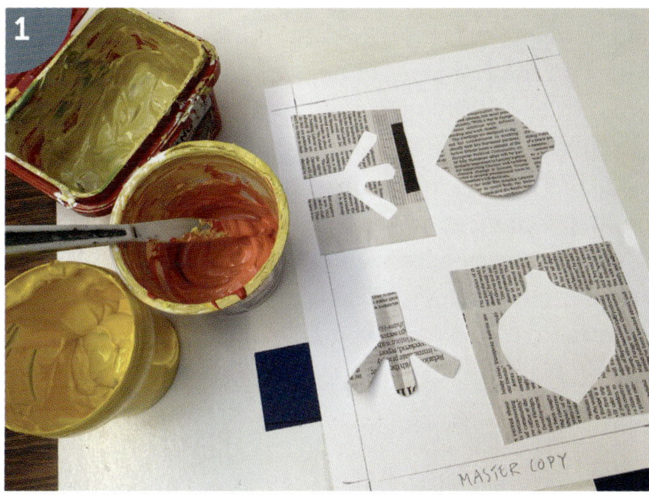

Use newspaper to cut positive and negative shapes. Work within a grid and split the design into quarters. Arrange the paper stencils on top of the master page.

Printing the first colour will pick up the paper stencils. Notice how strong the newspaper is. Choose a pale colour for the first print and don't be afraid to mix colours on the screen. Remove the stencils after printing.

When the first layer is dry, place a print in the registration stops and arrange the second layer of stencils on top.

For the second colour choose one that will enhance the first print. In this case a blue complements the under orange. Notice the interesting overlapping colours that appear.

When arranging the third layer of stencils, take care to distribute them in the quarter formation to get the best printed results. You can reuse previous stencils too.

Print the third colour. Notice the depth of colour you can achieve with three layers. I have used a purple that works with the yellow tints of the first layer.

MULTIMEDIA STENCILS

There are many different stencil alternatives that can be used to mask the screen and create a print. Below I have detailed some of the favourites that I often use together to create a monoprint print or to generate textured backgrounds to overlay a photo silkscreen print.

Start collecting suitable multimedia printing materials, such as plants. Ferns work well as they have interesting outline shapes. It's a good idea to press any flowers or leaves before use so that the screen can pick them up more easily. Look out for interesting waste packaging too: it's surprising what you can find. Textile textures that have a lace pattern or heavy weave can similarly provide great effects.

A selection of flat textured surfaces that you can use to block out the screen. Look for leaves with interesting outlines and press organic material prior to printing.

Newspaper is a strong all-rounder for paper stencils and can easily be torn or cut into shape. Soft edges can be combined with cut silhouettes.

Newsprint

Newsprint is a great all-rounder and can be cut or torn into interesting shapes. You can certainly exploit this by folding sheets into all kinds of concertinas and fans. Take your scissors and release your inner Matisse!

Try cutting reflecting patterns or a line of little characters, animals or birds. Newsprint stencils can be removed after printing, left to dry and then the process can be repeated on top of the initial print. This method can result in some surprising patterns and depth.

Torn newsprint is also very interesting as you get some lovely textured edges when you print.

Plant materials

You will need to experiment if you want to print using foliage. Leaves, particularly those with a detailed edge such as ferns, give the best results. I have tried both fresh and pressed and both seem to work well. You basically need to get the leaf to pick up on the screen in the same way as it would with a paper stencil, which will initially give you a silhouette.

Be aware that if you want to pick up the leaf veins and textured details you need to remove the wet leaf from the screen and put it back down on the paper wet side down.

This is more akin to relief printing. Obviously, you can't do this straight away and it only works for one print. I tend to have a stack of prints on the go and mix and match the botanicals. More information on this subject will be found in Chapter 4.

Waste products

Countless different flat wastepaper and plastic products can be found in the home or out in the shopping environment. You just need to look for them. Many make interesting silkscreen stencils and have been pre-cut from large stocks of paper. The waste around vinyl stickers can be stuck straight onto the screen and greaseproof paper, including the wax discs used in jam making. A visit to your local Scrapstore will turn up countless discarded shapes.

Woven fabrics

Very fine textiles can be picked up on the screen and printed. You may find that a heavy deposit of ink is laid down, however, in which case you will need to leave the print to dry for 24 hours. Textiles can also add a textured dimension to a print.

Combine woven fabrics, paper waste and plants to create some interesting designs.

Plants that lie flat with serrated edges like these ferns make great silhouettes. If you layer the leaves, you can create some stunning prints.

PROJECT: MULTIMEDIA PRINTS

This project gives you the chance to try combining different materials including plants and textiles using the pick-up method of silkscreen printing. You will be using your A4 masked screen and previous materials and equipment. Use the same screen and inks as in the previous chapter and have newspaper available to dry stencil material. Make sure you have plenty of wastepaper as this can get messy.

Layers of colour and texture appear in this print, which uses a range of silhouettes including leaves, paper waste and lace.

Method

Experiment using fresh or pressed plants under your screen and print a series of abstract monoprints. Cut them to shape if necessary and lay them on the printing board. Work from light to dark ink or dark to light ink. It's interesting to see how light opaque colours can overlay on darker backgrounds.

Consider the design space and experiment with design placements. You will need to leave prints to dry between colours. Make a collection of flat textured surfaces that you can use to block out the screen. Look for leaves with interesting outlines and press organic material prior to printing.

EQUIPMENT AND MATERIALS

You will require a masked screen, baseboard and squeegee. Collect and assemble a range of flat stencil-making materials including plants, newspaper and thin textiles.

* Thick printing paper (200–300gsm)
* Flat stencil materials, such as plants and textiles
* Craft knife
* Squeegee
* Ink (four colours including white) and printing medium
* Masking tape
* Hairdryer
* Palette knives
* Paintbrushes and sponges
* Apron and rubber gloves

Place flat materials under the screen on the baseboard. Make sure that they do not overlap and arrange them in blocks with space between the shapes

View the print area by laying the screen down and rearrange the shapes to fit the screen mask.

Flood the screen and pull the squeegee over the screen with the first colour.

The materials are picked up on the underside screen.

Printing may be uneven depending on the thickness of the materials and you may have to apply pressure to get the ink to flood through small areas.

Remove the stencil material and clean screen. When the first colour is dry, repeat the process with new materials.

Print a second colour. Reuse stencils by placing them ink side down on the paper before printing. Remove the stencil materials carefully and lay aside, ink side up

SILKSCREEN USING FILLERS, DRAWING FLUIDS AND WAX CRAYONS

Screen filler is a coloured fluid. When applied to the screen it dries to a permanent water-resistant finish. Filler can be used on its own and painted lines or textures will remain on the white of the paper when the stencil is printed. It resists ink and will not wash away when the screen is cleaned with water. As a result it requires a specific chemical remover so the screen can be reclaimed for further use.

Fillers are generally used for filling in pinholes on photo stencils. The solution is highly pigmented and you need to be careful when applying it to the screen. Wear a good pair of overalls as it will not come off clothing. I use it very sparingly and make sure to scoop up any residual filler with a spatula and return it to the bottle.

Combining filler with a water-based drawing fluid or water-based wax crayon takes simple hand-printed stencils to a new level. It enables you to work in the positive, so that whatever you paint or draw on the screen will print. The process depends on the filler being impervious to water and the painting and drawing medium dissolvable in water.

Fillers are also a great way of adding hand-painted text to a poster or card. The downside of the technique, however, is that it can be difficult to paint fine detail as you are restricted to using paintbrushes and the texture of the mesh can be quite coarse. Another issue is that you can't wash or remove the filler from the mesh once you've painted it on, so you might want to practise painting filler onto paper first to get the hang of the solution.

The following three methods detail different ways of using fillers, drawing fluids and wax resist.

Project: Filler-only stencils

This technique uses only filler. Before starting your design, it is useful to consider background colours as well as other printing techniques that can be printed first. You could, for example, print a couple of paler block colours and print your filler design on top.

Drawing fluid and filler enable you to create beautiful linear hand-painted stencils.

Filler stencils block out the screen and all the open areas print.

Application of filler

Create a printable area on your screen with masking tape. This will be your design area.

Start with the open screen and prepare your design. Work on a flat table and have pencils, paintbrushes and water at hand. I prefer to place and tape artwork under the screen and draw the design through onto the surface of the well of the screen. As you are working in the positive, there is no need to invert the design.

Before applying the filler, lift the screen clear of the design, otherwise it will leak through the screen on to the artwork below. A couple of coins placed underneath the screen frame will be enough to lift it clear. Mix the filler in the bottle before use and carefully paint out the design. Make sure you apply the filler with an even thickness: if it is too thick it will seep through the screen. The filler dries very quickly too, so make sure you wash the brush when you have finished with it. Also note that it can dry very hard on the lid of the container, so make sure you keep this clean too.

Fillers can be applied to the screen using card or a brush. You should also, however, try to experiment with different soft tools such as foam brushes and feathers. You can also use stencils or textures by, for example, soaking lace in a filler and applying it to the screen.

Leave the painted design to dry before printing. Try mixing ink on the screen to create a multicoloured print. Flood the screen with the top colour and print. The filler will successfully block out the screen, revealing the design.

To remove the stencil, place the screen on a flat surface covered with newspaper. Brush the appropriate stencil remover into the screen, front and back, and leave to stand for 15 minutes. Keep rubbing until the filler starts to break down and rinse with hot water.

EQUIPMENT AND MATERIALS

* Screen – clean and unmasked
* Baseboard
* Squeegee
* Palette knife (square cut)
* Screen filler
* Filler remover
* A range of paintbrushes
* Ink (two or three colours)
* Textured materials
* Soft pencil
* Printing paper
* Masking tape

PRINTING TIPS

You need to remember that whatever you paint will not print!

Filler can be applied with all kinds of drawing and painting equipment. Make sure you wash brushes immediately after use.

Remove the filler with an appropriate cleaner. It may take some time for the stencil to part company with the mesh.

Project: Drawing fluid/wax crayon and filler stencils

You will be working in the positive for this method so whatever you paint will print. Decide how you want to add qualities such as texture and tone. You can also add texture by printing with the drawing fluid.

Water-based wax crayons are a useful addition that can be used in conjunction with the fluid as they also will resist the filler and can be removed with the drawing fluid. The wax crayon method is a great way of getting that hand-drawn feel in your stencil and adds another dimension to prints as you can add shade and broken lines to the design.

The drawing fluid method combines water-based fluid with water-resistant filler and enables you to make linear drawings.

You can also use the crayons on top of a textured surface to make a rubbing on the screen, which the filler will pick up.

Simply paint or draw the water-based drawing fluid/wax crayon on the screen first to create your design. Let it dry and then screen a thin layer of filler over the top of the painted design. When the filler is dry, simply dissolve the drawing fluid/wax away with a wet sponge to reveal the painted design. If you make a mistake with the drawing fluid, you can remove it with water and start again.

After printing remove the filler in the usual way and clean the screen.

EQUIPMENT AND MATERIALS

* Screen – clean and unmasked
* Baseboard
* Squeegee
* Palette knife (square cut)
* Screen filler and drawing fluid
* Filler remover
* Ink
* A range of paintbrushes
* Textured materials
* Soft pencil
* Printing paper
* Masking tape
* Worked-up design
* Water-based crayons
* Water and sponge

1 Create your design on a master sheet. Here some motifs have been collaged, stuck on a piece of A4 paper and placed within a 1cm border on the page.

2 The collaged design is placed under the screen in the printing position. To keep everything in position you can secure both the design and screen with tape.

3 Using a soft pencil, the design and border is traced through onto the screen.

4

Remove the design sheet and prop the screen so it does not touch the table (otherwise the drawing fluid will smudge). The design is then outlined using the water-based crayon and the blue drawing fluid. The wax crayon is good for capturing shadows and fine lines.

5

Don't over-paint and leave pools of fluid on the surface. Leave the painting to dry overnight or you can speed this up with a hairdryer. Note that it's difficult to partially remove the fluid, so if you make a mistake, it's best to wash off and start again. When the drawing fluid is dry tape the print area with masking tape.

6

Apply a thin layer of filler at the top of the screen, making sure that it is wide enough to cover the masked area.

7

Using a squeegee, pull the filler across the painted design. Try to do this is in one pull. Leave the screen to dry in a flat position. All surplus filler should be returned to the bottle as soon as possible. Clean the filler top before replacing the cap.

8

Wash the screen with a hosepipe or wet sponge. This will dissolve the drawing fluid and leave the open areas of the design ready to print.

9

When the screen is dry, place the screen on the printing board and register with the printing paper. Print the design in the usual way or print under-colours first, using paper stencils, and apply the filler design on top.

Method: Reduction print using filler

This method uses filler only and works on the basis that you are continually blocking out the same printing screen to build up a design. It works in the same way as reduction lino printing, moving through the lightest colour to the darker layer by removing areas of the screen using the filler and printing subsequent colours. You need a good design to refer to and a specific colour scheme.

This method enables you to make a multicoloured print using one screen. The downside of this technique is that you are committed to printing whatever you have blocked out on the screen. There is no turning back and very little room for error.

When you have masked off the screen and printed the first colour, you will continue to use the same registration marks for subsequent colours. It is important to keep the screen locked in the clamps throughout.

Image of reduction filler print.

EQUIPMENT AND MATERIALS

* Paintbrushes
* Screen – clean and unmasked
* Baseboard
* Squeegee
* Palette knife (square cut)
* Screen filler
* Filler remover
* Textured materials
* Three coloured inks: light, medium and dark
* Soft pencil
* Printing paper (decide how many prints you want in the edition)
* Masking tape

Design
Create a design on paper in four colours, including the white of the paper. Here three shades of green are used, each colour numbered from 1 (the white paper) to 4 (the dark green). I outlined the design on a separate piece of paper, numbering each colour section. I also created a pencil border.

Apply design to screen
Create a taped printing area with waterproof tape. Place the design under screen and copy the first colour with a soft pencil onto the screen.

Apply first layer of filler
With the screen flat but sightly lifted off the table, block out all areas numbered 2 with filler using a small paintbrush. Attach the screen to the printing table.

Print first colour – pale green
Position the paper under the screen and register with the painted stencil. Registration stops are added. Flood and print the first colour (pale green). After printing the screen is left in situ. This is important to ensure that the next colour registers. Do not remove the registration stops.

5

Apply second layer of filler
Place the paper design back under the screen and align it with the first colour. The second colour, olive green, numbered 3 on the design, is drawn on the screen and painted with the filler.

6

Print second colour – olive green
Place the paper in the registration stops on the baseboard. Flood the screen and print with the olive green. Note how the print has been designed to overprint on the first colour. After printing the screen is cleaned in position ready for the final filler layer.

7

Apply third layer of filler
Place the paper design back under the screen in the registration stops. The third dark green colour, number 4 on the design, is drawn on the screen and painted with the filler. Texture is added underneath the pot by sponging the filler on the screen.

8

Print third colour – dark green
Place the paper in the registration stops on the baseboard, Flood the screen and print with the dark green. This completes the print. Notice the textural detail on the table at the bottom of the pot.

Project: Using filler to create texture

This is a simple introduction to the filler technique. The aim is to discover the textural detail that can be created with flat materials that leave a printable mark on the screen.

Using the open screen area, apply different filler marks using a paintbrush or other tool that leaves a soft mark. Try using a stencil or soaking fabric in filler and printing on top of the screen. Let the filler dry before printing. Alternatively use two screens and print one on top of the other.

EQUIPMENT AND MATERIALS

This project uses your A4 masked screen and previous materials and equipment. Put together a collection of potential flat printing resources, such as plants, feathers, textiles and wallpaper.

* Clean screen – masked to A4
* Printing paper
* Cutting knife
* Squeegee
* Ink (two or three colours) and printing medium
* Screen filler and filler remover
* Masking tape
* Palette knives
* Paintbrushes and sponges
* Textural materials
* Apron and rubber gloves

Printed design made with filler.

Project: Positive and negative grid

This project will create a two-colour print combining paper stencil and filler printing methods. Use paper stencils to create an under-colour and create a grid design that fits on top featuring positive and negative motifs.

Measure out a grid with six or nine equal squares. Draw this out on paper first. Create a series of small designs within each square, repeating the motifs if you wish. Fill each square, work in the positive and negative and in black and white only. Each motif should sit next to a positive or negative shape.

EQUIPMENT AND MATERIALS

* Clean screen
* Printing paper
* Cutting knife
* Squeegee
* Ink (two colours) and printing medium
* Screen filler and filler remover
* Masking tape
* Palette knives
* Paintbrushes
* Apron and rubber gloves
* Drawing fluid
* A worked-up design that fits within the printing area

Grid motifs are an easy way of creating a design for filler and drawing fluid stencils.

Transfer the design to the screen by placing the design under the mesh and trace through with a soft pencil.

Paint the drawing fluid on the screen in the design area. Decant the fluid into a small container.

Mask around the design with masking tape. Screen over the area with filler using a squeegee.

When the filler is dry remove the tape. Use a wet sponge to remove the drawing fluid and reveal the design.

Create a paper stencil to print a contrasting background colour and, when dry, print the grid design on top.

CHAPTER 4

SILKSCREEN MONOPRINT AND MONOTYPE

Monoprint and monotype are two terms that often cause confusion in the world of print due to their similar names and techniques. However, they represent distinct processes and outcomes.

The significant distinction between the two printmaking terms is that a monoprint is a method of creating a one-of-a-kind artwork that contains elements that are repeated in other prints. For example, you might use the same paper stencils but print them using different colours or you may incorporate a photo stencil image and repeat across a series of prints.

Monotypes are, however, 'unique' prints that are generally painted on the screen as a one-off art print and not repeated. Monotype silkscreens are generally hand painted and are often unstructured and spontaneous.

Screen print monoprint and monotypes combine a wide range of techniques and are a very accessible way of experimenting with the silkscreen process to produce exclusive prints. You don't need to rely on any elaborate stencil methods, and you can use a range of water-based painting materials with the acrylic printing base you have used in previous chapters. The finished prints have a beautiful smooth quality and luminous colours.

The process can incorporate photo stencils too and direct methods that enable you to paint and draw on top of the mesh and screen the design through with a certain level of accuracy. I often use one-off painterly prints that blend photo stencil, drawing, paper stencils and textural rubbings.

The direct painting process requires a degree of speed and gestural mark making. I use my sketchbook drawings to inform my prints, and I may print several layers on top of one another, making design decisions as the print progresses.

Monoprint or monotype can also be combined with any other surface decoration including collage, painting, lino and block printing.

There is no order of printed layers, although I tend to work from lighter through to mid- and finally darker tones. Typically I have several monoprints on the go at the same time and use the same elements, but not necessarily in the the same order or in the same place on the paper. I can achieve this by removing and repositioning stencils or making under drawings or paintings as initial layers.

From sketchbook to print.

Hand painted monoprint.

OVERVIEW

There are no right or wrong ways of using these techniques and you may find that you are particularly drawn to one as it suits your way of working. There is a lot to experiment with too, and you can continue to overprint, redraw and rework in much the same way you might modify a painting or collage.

All the methods described in this chapter involve water-based materials including paint, crayons and graphite, which are applied to the well of the screen and printed through using screen binder.

Large areas of colour are applied with a brush. Prints can get quite wet and may need leaving overnight to dry before applying further layers. Water-based materials are easily removed from the screen with a soft cloth and warm water. Remember that acrylic paint can dry and is then difficult to remove, so don't delay in removing it from the screen after printing.

In the course of this chapter we will cover the following methods:

* Direct drawing and painting onto a silkscreen
* Multicoloured paper stencils
* Combining both printing techniques to produce textured and layered prints

Each process has a specific list of materials and equipment detailed at the start of each technique. Use a masked screen with registration stops in place and have a bucket of water and towel at the ready to clean and dry inbetween print pulls. Do not remove the screen from the hinges. If you keep it in place, it is easier to maintain the registration when applying second print layers.

As you will be layering several coats of ink through the screen, it's advisable to use 300gsm paper. Be careful when drawing on your screen and avoid chalky charcoal and pastels as they are very abrasive and can damage screen

One-of-a-kind monoprints painted directly on the screen.

mesh. I would also keep away from highly pigmented inks, including Indian ink, as they stain the screen and are difficult to remove.

The following provides information on the properties of all drawing and painting materials used throughout this chapter:

Screen binder

This is the essential transparent printing medium that will be used to transfer the designs through the screen and onto the printing paper. It will also seal any painting or drawing medium applied to the screen.

It is also used in conjunction with acrylic paint if you are painting directly on the screen with these inks (see Chapter 2).

Paper

Monoprinting can leave the paper very wet, so use a heavy-duty cartridge paper with a weight of 300gsm. Don't be tempted to use a textured watercolour paper as you will get uneven printing. Prints may need to dry overnight between print layers.

Texture

Textured rubbings can also be added to all the methods described. I have a large collection of surfaces for use in my prints including collograph plates, wallpaper and plants. You can combine this technique with stencils cut from paper or any collected plants.

Acrylic printing ink

I prefer to keep and mix my ink in small pots with separate brushes and have them close to where I am working. I also keep a pot of water handy to clean the brushes.

Test your inks for colour beforehand to make sure you have the right consistency – not too runny or too thick. If you are printing multilayers, think about how you can add opacity to your colours by adding white paint to block out part of a strong under-colour and give your print depth.

Make sure you have plenty of cleaning cloths at hand and clean towels to dry the screen in-between printing. There is plenty of speed required in this process.

Watercolour paints and gouache

These are great media to use and very flexible as they do not contain any acrylic, so you can take your time painting them on the screen and leave them to dry. The colour options are far greater too and you can blend colour more easily than with acrylic ink.

Once they are painted on the screen they sit on the top of the mesh and are activated when the transparent screen medium is squeegeed across. This dissolves them into the medium and they can be pushed through the screen and printed. Leave them in a palette and mix them with water as you would if painting onto paper with various dilutions.

Watercolours can also be used in the same way and give great depth to your prints. You can also use watercolours in conjunction with other media. Don't clean them off the palette, but let them dry hard and store them.

Graphite drawing sticks

These come in different grades. Choose a soft stick such as 2B to draw on your screen, but avoid anything softer as it can stain the screen. You can use the point or side of the stick to create different tones. Apply screen binder over the top and pull the image through the screen.

Watercolour pencils

Choose very soft pencils with lots of pigment. Keep the point blunt and rounded, otherwise you might tear the screen. Draw directly on the screen, perhaps spraying some water to dissolve the pigment to give a painterly effect.

Water-based wax crayons

Use these as you would on paper. The crayons are soft and don't damage the screen, so you can use them sharp.

SCREEN PAINTING WITH ACRYLIC INK

When you are using this method for the first time it is useful to have some resources to refer to or an idea of imagery and what colours you are going to use. All this needs to be collected at the start along with a bucket of water, cleaning cloth and towel to wash and dry the screen inbetween prints. The technique uses acrylic colours mixed with screen binder, which you paint directly into the well of the screen.

Painted monoprints can be overprinted much in the same way as a painting can be overpainted to enhance colour and detail.

EQUIPMENT AND MATERIALS

* Clean screen (masked as demonstrated in Chapter 2)
* Squeegee
* Bucket of water and cleaning cloths
* Acrylic paint mixed with printing binder 50:50
* Printing paper 300gsm
* Palette knives
* Paintbrushes, soft pencil and water-based crayon
* Water and cleaning cloths
* Imagery, such as sketchbooks

Method

This method uses acrylic ink that is mixed with binder and painted directly on top of the screen with a paintbrush. The design is then pushed through the screen using the squeegee onto printing paper placed on the baseboard below. Speed is of the essence and it suits a quick expressive working style.

It's important to register the screen and printing paper before you start. Once you get started and have added the registration marks they can be kept in place for subsequent prints if you don't remove the screen.

Register the prints using the method discussed in Chapter 2. Keeping the screen attached to the baseboard during and after cleaning will also enable the next layer to be added on top using the same registration. Decide how many layers you want to print; this technique can be very organic in that you might not end up with what you imagined. I generally apply pale colours first and decide to add subsequent darker or lighter colours as the print progresses.

Transferring the image

Place resource imagery under or near the screen in the print area. The image can be transferred with a pencil or water-based crayon to make outlines and marks directly on the screen. Whether you are adding line or painting ink on top of the screen, try to imagine you are working in layers.

Whatever you paint on the screen first will lie underneath anything you put on top and generally print first. Apply print binder to any areas of the design you want to remain as the white of the paper. If you are going to print a second layer and want to keep elements of the print underneath, apply binder to the mesh that corresponds to the printed areas that you want to maintain.

Painting

When painting the image on the screen it's important to work quickly as the ink will dry very quickly and block the screen. I try to complete my monoprints in ten to fifteen minutes before printing. If I am adding marks or outlines, I make these first as there is no urgency to draw swiftly onto the screen, so you can take your time over this. You can even remove the screen from the printing table and work elsewhere.

This process tends to favour abstract painted imagery and large gestural marks. It's essential to cover all the mesh with ink or printing binder when you are working.

If you leave the screen mesh open in any large areas, you will get a streaky, chaotic print with blended colours. If it's a very hot day I add a retarder to my ink, which helps the ink to stay open on the mesh for longer.

Printing

When you have completed the painted design, apply a very thin layer of screen fluid to the top of the screen with a paintbrush. If you have used a drawing underneath, remember to remove this before adding your printing paper. To print squeegee this fine layer across the screen, dragging all the painted ink across in a strong pull. You can employ a further pull, which can release more ink and a stronger print.

Cleaning the screen

Remove all the excess printing ink from the screen with a plastic spatula. Wash the screen with a cloth and warm water as soon as possible on both sides and dry with a clean towel. You don't need to remove the screen from the board and you are then ready to go again.

Transferring an image onto the screen before painting or drawing with a crayon

Lift the screen clear off the baseboard when painting.

Pull a thin layer of binder across the painted design with the squeegee.

DRAWING WITH GRAPHITE

Most water-based materials can be used to draw on the top of the screen and the image created is picked up and deposited on the paper in the printing process. Graphite sticks are a great example of an accessible material as they come in different weights and can be used to make direct as well as sketchy lines on the screen.

The graphite dissolves easily in the water-based screen medium and picks up textures if you place the screen on top of a rough surface when drawing. Graphite produces a wide range of lovely silvery tones and you can apply colour at the same time.

Method

Make your drawing in the well of the screen. Use the graphite on the point as well as the side to capture texture and tone in your image. The original artwork can be placed underneath the screen to capture the image and to arrange how it fills the screen. This can be done at a worktable before transferring to the printing bed.

Printing

Place a bead of silkscreen printing binder at the top of the screen and squeegee across the image in the usual way. Leave it for 30 seconds to penetrate the screen before printing.

Coloured backgrounds

A coloured background can be created by adding colour to the printing ink.

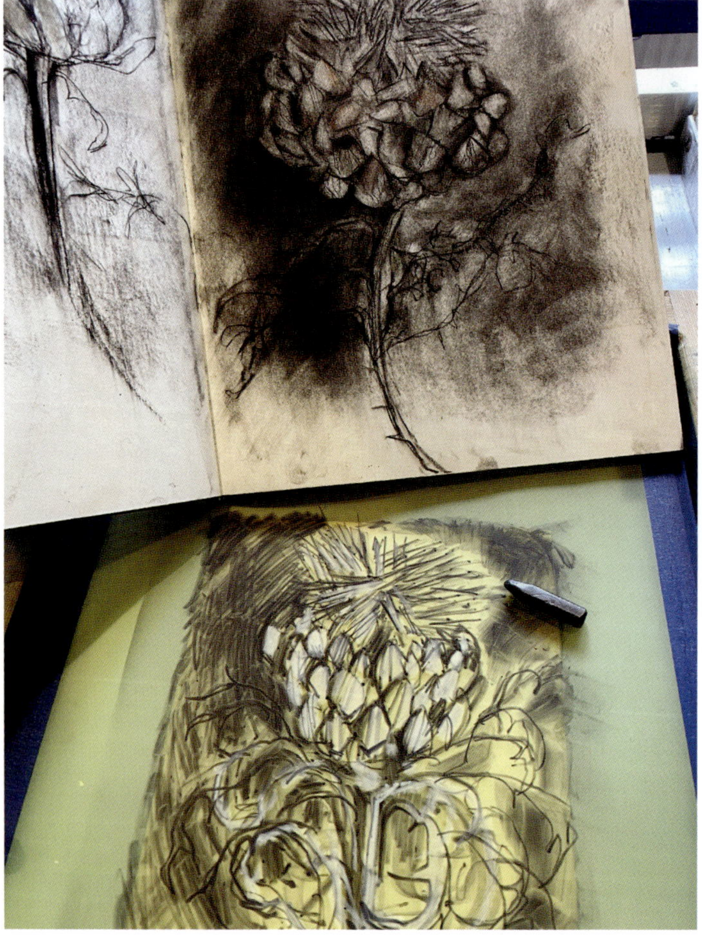

Graphite produces lovely silvery prints and can be combined with paint and crayon.

EQUIPMENT AND MATERIALS

* Clean screen (masked as demonstrated in Chapter 2)
* Squeegee
* Bucket of water and cleaning cloths
* 2B graphite stick
* Printing paper 300gsm
* Screen fluid
* Water and cleaning cloths
* Palette knife
* Reference material/sketchbook

When printing make a double pull to get as much of the image as possible to print through the screen. Do not flood the screen again when undertaking this.

Carefully draw using a graphite stick on the top of the screen mesh. Paint or sponge water over the graphite to achieve a painterly effect.

PAINTING WITH WATERCOLOURS

This is a variation on the painting technique discussed at the beginning of the chapter. You are replacing the acrylic inks with watercolour pigment.

The effect is subtle in that it replicates a watercolour effect. The colour is much more transparent and the finished print maintains the brushstrokes. When experimenting with this technique, make sure that the paint is not too wet and runny. Gouache also works very well. I combine this technique with wax and graphite drawings as it gives a soft background with more depth. As with the graphite technique above, the paint is sealed when the print binder is applied.

EQUIPMENT AND MATERIALS

* Clean screen (masked as demonstrated in Chapter 2)
* Squeegee
* Bucket of water and cleaning cloths
* Palette of watercolours
* Printing paper 300gsm
* Pot of water
* Selection of paintbrushes
* Screen fluid
* Water and cleaning cloths
* Palette knife

Water-based paints give more flexibility when printing and can be applied to the screen in the same way as acrylic paint.

Method

Mix paint in a palette and apply to the screen with paint brushes. Make sure it doesn't drip through the screen. Imagine you are painting a fine layer of paint on fabric. You will find that you can layer the paint and mix colours on the screen. You can also add graphite. If the watercolour is left to dry completely before printing you can avoid the possibility of the watercolour paint bleeding when printing. You will need to leave the screen flat to dry and the process can be speeded up with a hairdryer.

Printing

Place a bead of screen-printing fluid at the top of the screen and squeegee over the design. Leave for 30 seconds before printing. A double pull will increase the colour picked up in the print.

Watercolour paint can be left after application without fear of becoming dried-in on the screen.

Watercolour monoprints retain the transparency of the paint.

WATER-BASED WAX CRAYONS

Water-based crayons can be used very successfully in the monoprinting process and can be combined with all the direct drawing and painting techniques described in this chapter. There are lots of different ways of applying them and they can be used to add fine lines, expressive marks and outlines. They also pick up texture and you can make a rubbing with them through the screen onto a textured surface placed underneath the screen.

When used on their own it's a good idea to slightly moisten the screen. This helps dissolve the water-based wax into the screen and improves the quantity of pigment deposited on the screen. You can also first squeegee printing binder across the screen and draw directly onto the surface before printing.

Wax crayons can also be used to outline images and add detail to the acrylic or watercolour painting methods. Some crayon pigments are stronger than others, so it's best to experiment and make some examples before you start.

Crayons can also add tonal variations using a single colour, such as sepia or black, that can be picked up very successfully during printing. Try using the side of the crayon too or popping the crayon in water before drawing to dissolve the pigment.

Water-based wax crayons can add lines and textures to a monoprint.

EQUIPMENT AND MATERIALS

* Clean screen (masked as demonstrated in Chapter 2)
* Squeegee
* Bucket of water and cleaning cloths
* Water-based wax crayons
* Printing paper 300gsm
* Pot of water
* Selection of paintbrushes
* Screen fluid
* Water and cleaning cloths
* Palette knife

Method

Place your inspirational material either under or on top of the screen. It may be wise to cover it with a sheet of acetate to avoid it getting wet. Slightly moisten the screen before you start and transfer the image using a palette of wax crayons. Make the most of the mark-making attributes of the material.

When you have finished, add a bead of print binder across the top of the screen image, making sure you have enough to flood across the image with the squeegee. When you have squeegeed the print binder across the screen, leave it in situ for a couple of minutes and let the binder soak into the wax crayon.

Make sure you place paper underneath the screen in the registration stops. Add some more binder at the top of the screen and this time apply print pressure and print. This process can be repeated to enhance the colour, but be careful not to move the printing paper on the screen or you may get a misaligned print.

Try working in monocolour. Black crayons capture a range of tones and mark-making and can be used alongside graphite.

A sketchbook can be placed next to the drawing or underneath the screen.

The screen binder dissolves the wax crayon and deposits colour from the screen onto the paper.

Before and after crayon and graphite monoprint.

TEXTURAL MONOPRINTS

Texture can be added to prints in lots of different ways, but I think that silkscreen monoprinting offers lots of creative possibilities. I enjoy adding textural elements to my prints, whether that is broken and distressed lines, rubbings taken from unusual surfaces or the application of tonal mark-making.

Method

Texture can be worked into the design to enhance a background or draw attention to a specific element. I actively look for textures to collect and use in my prints and these include such varied items as old collagraph plates, textiles, wood surfaces and netting.

When applying any textures these should be placed under the screen. You then imagine that you are making a brass rubbing. Water-based wax crayons and graphite sticks are both fine for this as you can use the side of the material to get a good impression of the surface underneath. Strong crayon pigments work best. You can either print the textures on top of an existing print or add printing ink over the top so that it sits behind the textural area when printed.

Screen care when using textures

You will find that the screen mesh is a great surface for drawing and painting. However, you must look after it and avoid using anything sharp or too abrasive that can easily slash or pinhole the mesh.

Printing texture

Printing uses the same methods as in previous materials. Add a small bead of printing binder, squeegee over and leave for 30 seconds before printing. If you apply too much crayon the pigment can be difficult to remove from the screen after printing.

Texture can be introduced to monoprints using wax crayon, which can be used together with acrylic paint.

EQUIPMENT AND MATERIALS

* Clean screen (masked as demonstrated in Chapter 2)
* Squeegee
* Bucket of water and cleaning cloths
* Collection of textures
* Printing paper 300gsm
* Water-based wax crayons
* Pot of water
* Selection of paintbrushes
* Screen fluid
* Water and cleaning cloths
* Palette knife

PAPER-STENCIL MONOTYPES

Paper stencils are very versatile and can be carefully arranged to create prints with depth and variation using the same elements. Imagery can also be built using a combination of stencil and paint to block out and enhance a design.

EQUIPMENT AND MATERIALS

* Clean screen (masked as demonstrated in Chapter 2)
* Squeegee
* Bucket of water and cleaning cloths
* Stencil paper
* Printing paper 300gsm
* Scissors, craft knife and cutting board
* Acrylic ink (mixed and in a selection of colours)
* Pot of water
* Selection of paintbrushes
* Screen Fluid

Method

Changing the colour of a layer but using the same stencils can have a huge effect on the final print outcome. These prints use the same stencils, but some have been removed and replaced in a new position, and the colour has been mixed on the screen to change the final print.

This method of altering and repositioning stencils introduces variety and complexity into each print. By experimenting with the layering and colour mixing directly on the screen, you can achieve unique and varied results in each iteration of the print.

Make stencils

You can plan a design or choose several abstract elements and cut them out of stencil paper or newsprint.

Printing

Use the stencils to block out the screen and work from light to dark printing inks. Reposition the stencils to block out colours that lie underneath and add some hand-painting. Aim for two or three layers.

This two-layered print uses hand painting and collaged paper stencils to break up the bowl shape and add depth and highlights to the fruit that crowns the top.

This print uses several large stencil blocks that are printed, then repositioned to create a print with lots of depth.

COMBINING STENCILS, PAINT AND CRAYON

This is my favourite monoprinting method as it combines all the approaches discussed in one print. My attitude is very playful and once again speed is important to me. It's important to build up the depth of colour through a layered print system and ensure that you don't obliterate the detail or print contrast, which is easy to do if you start with dark colours.

Method

Start with simple paper stencils and print light colours first, maintaining the white paper. I tend to design within the print frame and call on my memory for ideas or imagery from my sketchbook. I then move on to adding painted colour and finally mark-making and texture.

I have several prints on the go at the same time and this gives me the chance to alter the colour if I want to make an adjustment.

Combining hand-cut stencils and hand drawing in one print.

EQUIPMENT AND MATERIALS

* Clean screen (masked as demonstrated in Chapter 2)
* Squeegee
* Bucket of water and cleaning cloths
* Acrylic paint (two to three colours) mixed 50:50 with print binder
* Printing paper 300gsm
* Water-based wax crayons
* Stencil paper and cutting tools
* Pot of water
* Selection of paintbrushes
* Screen fluid
* Water and cleaning cloths
* Palette knife
* Textural materials

Cut stencils

Stencils are cut out of paper or acetate; they are positioned in the printing area and the first colour is printed using the pick-up method of printing. Stencils can be moved around during the process too and a second print pull applied.

Printing

This is a chance to mix ink on the screen and create colour variations. Simply smooth ink across the screen before flooding the screen. This will result in mixing the colour and producing interesting colour effects. Remove the stencils and clean the screen.

When the prints are dry a second colour can be applied with the stencils repositioned. Print the second layer by mixing colour on the screen again to create new shades. Remove the stencils and wash and dry the screen.

Painting and drawing

Use acrylic paint and wax crayon to outline the design and paint around and within the shapes. You will need to place a print underneath the screen as a visual aid, and cover it with acetate to protect it. Remove the acetate, apply screen fluid and print.

Stencils can be printed, removed and rearranged on the screen to create overlapping colours.

PROJECT: PORTRAIT SCREEN PAINTING USING CRAYON AND PAINT

This project provides an opportunity to experiment with paint and crayon to create unique prints. The subject matter is portraiture, which can be approached in various ways, such as selecting an iconic painting or photograph, working from life or creating an imaginary character.

Method

Combine crayon, paint and textural rubbings directly on the screen and then print.

Design

Place your design under the screen and draw through it using a soft pencil or crayon. Alternatively, use a mirror to create your own portrait and draw directly on the screen.

Add crayon and paint

Lift the screen off the baseboard while completing your painting. Add the texture and drawing first, followed by the paint.

Printing

Apply a small line of print binder to the top of the screen and print. A second pull will enhance the colour.

Crayon can be used to outline and added on top of the stencil printing as a final layer.

A simple combination of acrylic paint, wax crayon and texture is used in this print. Add wax crayon and texture first before applying the paint.

EQUIPMENT AND MATERIALS

* Clean screen (masked as demonstrated in Chapter 2)
* Squeegee
* Palette knife
* Selection of paintbrushes
* Bucket of water and cleaning cloths
* Acrylic paint mixed 50:50 with print binder
* Printing paper 300gsm
* Resources, such as photographs and sketchbook
* Water-based wax crayons
* Pot of water
* Screen fluid
* Water and cleaning cloths
* Textural materials

The printed wax colour is heightened when printed

CHAPTER 5

INTRODUCTION TO PHOTO SILKSCREEN

If you are intimidated by technical and sometimes time-consuming processes you might understandably choose to jump over this chapter, but if you persevere and are prepared to put some time and effort into experimenting with a few pieces of basic equipment you won't be disappointed. The photo silkscreen process will transform your approach to print and will enable you to make work that the other print methods described in this book cannot replicate.

I have been using the low-tech methods described in this chapter at home for many years with great success and with very basic and limited equipment.

Stencil making for photo silkscreen requires a transparency with an opaque design either painted or drawn on the surface. Alternatively, you can create a design on paper and photocopy it onto a translucent sheet or output a design from a computer. The process transfers the design onto the silkscreen using a photo emulsion that you apply to the screen in advance and expose to a UV light source.

My own approach to this method is mainly analogue as I aim to replicate my expressive drawing and mark-making without the use of a photocopier or computer. Hence, I tend to hand-paint and draw my stencils onto clear cellophane to the printable size.

There are of course lots of accessible ways of working and making stencils. I will explain the most popular methods and materials in this chapter alongside the technical requirements of coating, exposing and printing photo silkscreens.

Just a word of warning. Although this process isn't dangerous you do need to take care cleaning screens and wear protective clothing when removing the photographic emulsion from the screen. I would also recommend a power washer or jet wash to undertake this and it should preferably be done at an outside location. It can be difficult to remove stencils from screens that have high mesh counts, such as 120T, without a power washer.

You also need a dark, enclosed space to store your screens after coating, such as a cupboard, chest of drawers or wardrobe.

You can, of course, do most of the dirty work in the home bathroom and shower, but you need to be diligent in cleaning up to avoid contaminating surfaces and any textiles.

Photo silkscreen uses a UV photosensitive emulsion to transfer designs onto the screen.

Photo silkscreen print 'Lemons and Sardines'.

AN OVERVIEW OF THE PROCESS

Photo stencils are made using a UV light-sensitive liquid or emulsion, which is used to coat the back of the screen, and a stencil made from a sheet of acetate with a design that is either hand-painted or computer-generated. The stencil is referred to as the 'positive'.

Only a thin layer of emulsion is required. It penetrates the screen mesh and dries to a hard sheen that is sensitive to UV light. The screen should be kept in the dark while it dries and until you want to use it.

Once the screen has dried the stencil is placed on top of the light-sensitive emulsion and exposed to the UV light source. The stencil image is then recorded on the light-sensitive screen surface. Although the process is known as photo silkscreen, a camera is not involved in this method.

The stencil can be made on any clear or semi-clear surface, such as tracing paper, drafting film and acetate, including florists' acetate. The process is positive, so whatever you draw or paint on the surface will turn into a printable area when the screen is exposed to a UV light source. You need to make sure that your stencil designs have enough opacity to resist the light source, otherwise the light will creep through and the design will be lost during the exposure.

The exciting moment when your photo stencil is revealed on the screen.

Getting to grips with the stencil exposure is not difficult. You just need to bear in mind that where the emulsion is exposed to the UV light source a chemical reaction will take place, and it will harden and block the screen mesh. All the design areas where the light can't penetrate will remain unexposed.

After you have exposed the screen, it is developed using a cold shower or hose spray. All the unexposed areas of emulsion simply wash away revealing the printable image. This is the magical part of the process when you realise that you have essentially copied your image onto a silkscreen with the most basic of equipment.

The screen is left to dry before printing and prepared as in previous chapters. The emulsion resists water so is suitable for use with water-based inks. However, you will require a specialist emulsion remover to reclaim the screen after use.

A good deal of preparation is required before you get started with the photo silkscreen process. As well as pulling all the equipment and materials together you need to consider where you will undertake all the messy preparation and stencil wash-out. Consider different options. You might be able to use an outbuilding or sign up to a print studio first to try the process and look at how you can adapt it to a home environment. You may be able to share resources with another budding silkscreen printer.

All printing equipment remains the same and the exposure unit is easy to assemble. My first box was made from heavy-duty cardboard and a piece of Perspex.

Screens and mesh count for photo silkscreen

Make sure you have the right mesh count to undertake your design. Tiny details and lines can be lost if you have a low mesh count. The mesh number relates to how many threads there are per centimetre of mesh. Mesh that is suitable for printing onto fabric is around 43T, whereas 90T is suitable for paper. This isn't always the case, however, depending on the level of detail you may have in your artwork. I tend to work with higher mesh counts such as 120T to avoid losing the details in my prints. This can reduce the amount of ink that is laid down on the paper and can cause the screen to dry in quickly.

EQUIPMENT AND MATERIALS

- Screen (90 mesh count)
- Exposure box and UV light
- Screen emulsion coating trough
- Screen cleaning brush
- Palette knife (chisel shape)
- Photo emulsion
- Photo emulsion remover/de-coater solution
- Bucket of water and cleaning cloths
- Transparency with design
- Screen degreasing solution
- Masking tape
- Sheet of old card to cover the floor

Exposure unit

I recommend that you build a small exposure unit from a cardboard, plastic or wooden box. This could be completely makeshift, but if you get bitten by the process or are working in an educational environment, a more permanent hand-built container on wheels will be more flexible and safer to use.

I suggest that you find a box with strong walls that stands 50cm high, 75cm long and 50cm wide. A large plastic storage box would be suitable.

The UV light I recommend is a 30-watt UV LED black light, which operates in the UV-A range with a wavelength of 395–400nm (some models use 365–70nm). It has a working temperature of 40–65°C, so make sure you turn it off after use as it can get quite hot. The 30W UV light source that I use provides good coverage for stencils up to A3 in size, although I have been able to make larger exposures. (Recommended suppliers of UV light units are listed in the appendix.)

My preferred method of exposure is to direct the UV light source up through the stencil to the back of the coated screen. I do not suspend the light above the screen, and I do not stay in the room with an uncovered UV light source. The LED UV light source is placed flat in the middle of the box bottom. You will need to be near an electrical socket to operate it, so wheels make it easy to manoeuvre.

To complete the exposure unit a piece of toughened glass or strong Perspex covers the top, trapping the light unit inside. You need to be careful with the glass placement and ensure that it fits the box top with an overhang of 3–4cm. If you use glass make sure it is toughened, has rounded edges and corners and is at least 3mm thick. Although Perspex is more expensive it is safer to handle.

The electrical wire should be fed over the top of the box and under the Perspex, or a hole could be cut in the bottom to enable it to poke through at ground level and reach the electrical socket.

The screen and transparency fit together on top so you will also require a cover to protect your eyes during exposure; a blanket will do the trick. Covering the box during the exposure means that you can continue to work in the same space.

Ensure that there is good contact between the screen and transparency during the exposure period. If there is a slight gap between the two you will get an uneven exposure. A rubber cutting board is great for this with a few heavy books placed on top.

Photo emulsion

Liquid emulsion is the cheapest and easiest way of making photo stencils. There are lots of different brands to choose from. The direct emulsion comes in two solutions that are mixed to make the solution sensitive to UV light. Take care to wear gloves when mixing as the sensitizer has a powerful yellow stain. If the mixture is stored in a dark cool place, it should be acceptable to use for three months.

You will also need photo emulsion remover to remove the stencil and reclaim the screen when you have finished printing. Each brand of emulsion will have its own specific chemical remover, so don't assume that any brand of remover will do. You must also wear rubber gloves when using this chemical.

Coating trough

You will need a smooth metal coating trough into which the emulsion is poured to coat the screen. This should have removable end caps to make it easy to pour unused emulsion back into the pot. Troughs come in lots of different sizes. You will need one that covers the interior of the frame, but does not extend onto the frame.

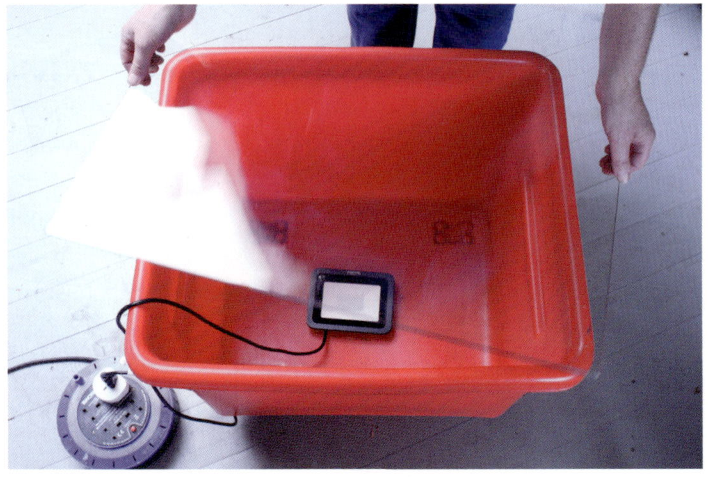

My handmade exposure unit consists of a plastic box on wheels. The UV light is placed at the bottom and a large piece of glass covers the top.

Troughs should be cleaned thoroughly after use including the cap ends, which tend to block and fall off, leaving a trail of emulsion everywhere. You can avoid this by temporarily taping them onto the trough ends.

Stencil film and mark-making

Any transparent material that will hold a mark or paint can be used to make a 'positive' for photo silkscreen. Florists' acetate is the cheapest, however tracing paper, inkjet transparencies as well as technical films are all suitable and their properties will be discussed below. Thicker acrylic paint-based pens work best on handmade positives, but I have experimented with all kinds of wet materials and crayons.

A wide range of acetates are available suitable for making hand-painted stencils.

HAND-PAINTED STENCILS

As an introduction to the technique we are going to make an A4 two-colour, simple hand-painted stencil on florists' acetate based on sketchbook imagery.

Method

Break down the image into two distinct layers by painting or drawing directly on the acetate. Each layer will be turned into a stencil.

Design

Outline the basic design in pencil on paper first so that it fits within the paper dimensions, adding as much detail as you require. This will provide the template for the painted acetates.

Stencil painting

Two sheets of A4 acetate are cut and labelled before painting. The bottom under-colour is painted with Indian ink and the top detail is drawn with an acrylic pen. Care should be taken to make sure that when printed the colours will match up.

Adding texture

When the ink and pen are dry, additional texture can be added by scratching with a craft knife.

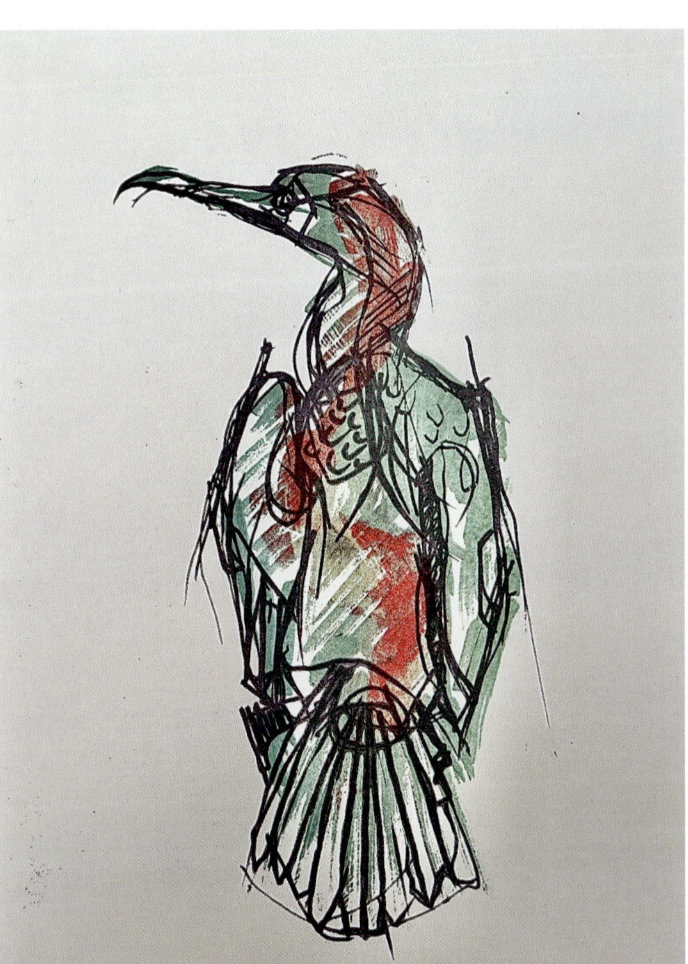

This two-colour stencil captures the texture of this iconic bird using two colours.

EQUIPMENT AND MATERIALS

* Transparent material (cellophane)
* Indian ink and acrylic paint pens
* Craft knife
* A4 drawing paper
* Pencil
* Paintbrushes
* Scissors
* Masking tape
* Light box (optional)
* Drawing inspiration

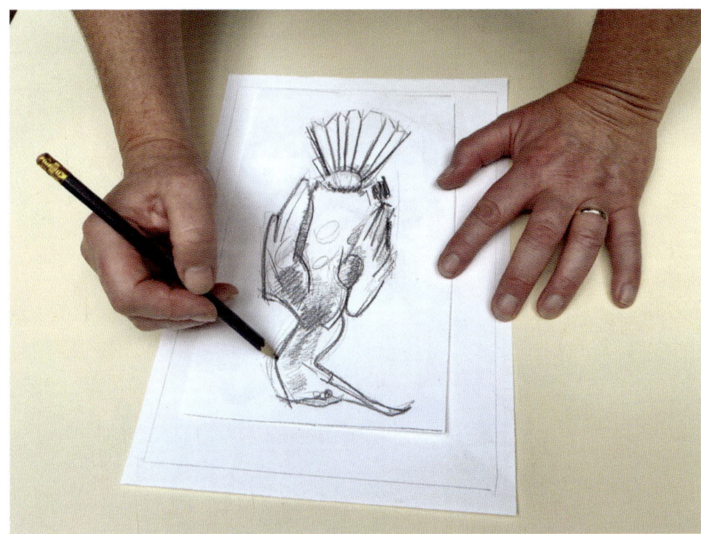

A quick pencil drawing on A4 paper to outline the design.

Stencils are painted in black ink and pen only. The marks should be as opaque as possible

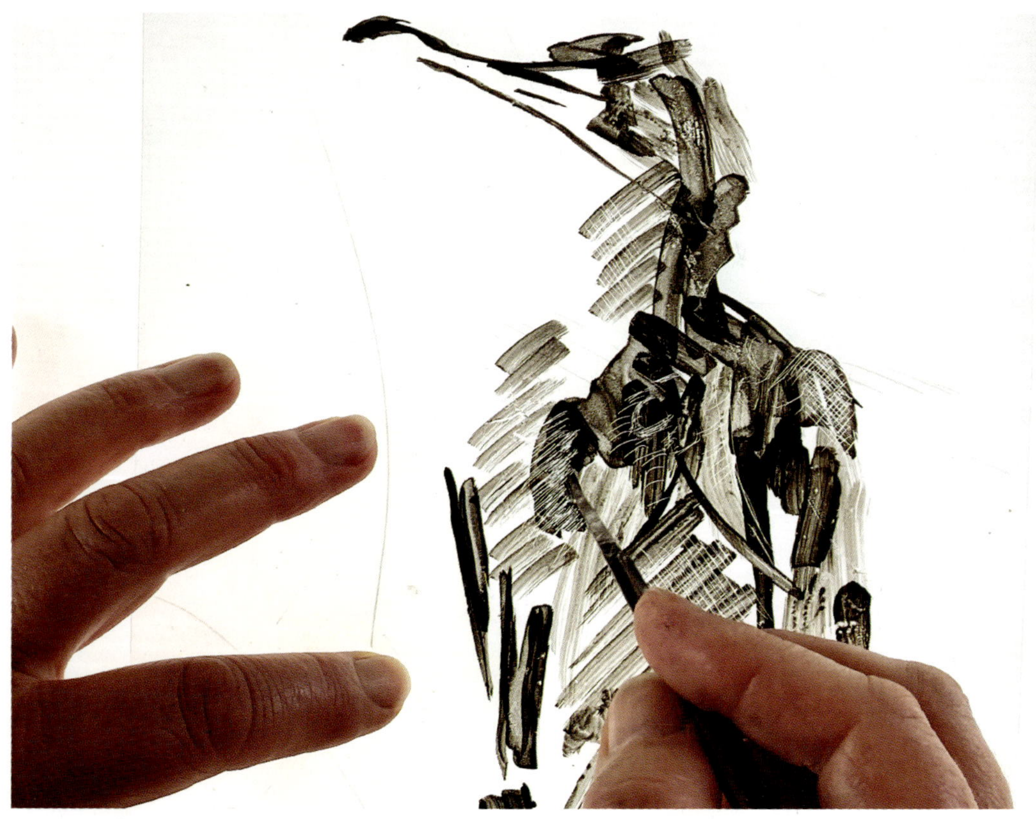

Try scratching at the paint when it's dry to reveal white lines and more detail.

SCREEN COATING

Method

Before making a photo stencil you need to ensure that the screen is free of grease, dust and so on. A degreaser solution is used to remove any residues, including fingerprints, that might prevent the emulsion adhering to the screen. Use the brush to work the degreaser into the screen on both sides with some water. Remove all residues. After degreasing the screen leave it to dry prior to coating with emulsion. Coating a screen is a one-person job, but there is quite a bit of cleaning up to do afterwards, so it is more efficient to coat a few screens at a time.

Mixing the photo emulsion

The emulsion comes in two parts that need to be mixed before use. The standard quantity that you buy will coat numerous screens, so consider this when you start using it. It will, however, keep in a cool dark place if the lid remains tightly fixed. I keep mine in a light-tight cupboard when mixed and it stays usable for up to four months.

The sensitizer comes in a small bottle and is dissolved in a quantity of water before adding it to the large container of emulsion. Wear rubber gloves and an apron as you don't want to sensitize your hands or clothing. Mix the two solutions together to create a homogeneous solution. I suggest that the mixture should be left for an hour before initial use to ensure that any air bubbles are dispersed.

Coating the screen with photo emulsion

Before you start make sure that you have everything at hand, and you are in a low-light area. Place some cardboard on the ground to protect the floor and make sure you have a damp cloth.

EQUIPMENT AND MATERIALS

* Screen (90 mesh count)
* Screen emulsion coating trough
* Mixing stick
* Hand protection
* Emulsion (2-part solution)
* Palette knife (chisel shape)
* Bucket of water and cleaning cloths

Use the coating trough to apply emulsion to the back of the screen. Make sure the trough fits within the mesh area and does not overlap the screen frame. Pour emulsion into the trough to a height of 3cm. Although you only use a small amount of emulsion you need to make sure that the trough is fully loaded across the gutter and runs smoothly over the mesh.

There are different methods of applying emulsion. I prefer to hold my screens with one hand and the trough in the other. Other printers lean the screen against a wall and hold the trough at either end with both hands.

The aim is to coat the back of the screen with a thin, smooth layer of emulsion. Start at the bottom of the screen, which is tilted at 45 degrees, and tilt the trough as well. Maintaining a good connection, pull the trough up to the top of the screen in a smooth motion. Try not to wobble

Make sure you wear protective clothing and disposable gloves when mixing the emulsion.

or change speed or you will achieve an uneven coat. Whichever way you perform this manoeuvre, it's probably the tensest part of the process as it's easy to get an uneven application of emulsion.

When you reach the top of the screen, tilt the trough backwards to enable the emulsion to run back into the gutter. At this point carefully put the trough down and remove any excess emulsion, using a square-cut palette knife, and replace it directly into the pot.

Wipe the edges of the screen with a damp cloth and remove any excess emulsion. Remove one of the trough ends and scrape the emulsion back into the pot. Wash the trough thoroughly afterwards and dry the screen vertically in a dark room.

Fill the trough with emulsion.

Starting at the bottom of the screen, tilt the trough, making sure the emulsion is evenly distributed across the edge.

Pull the trough up the screen and tilt at the top.

Clean the edges of the screen with the square palette knife.

SCREEN EXPOSURE

The exposure unit we are going to use will easily take stencils up to A3 in size. It is important that you have screens that can accommodate your size of stencil. Ensure that you have a warm room to dry the screen after exposure.

Method

Before you get started, make sure that you clean the glass or Perspex exposure surface. Any dust, stray hair, dirty fingerprints or similar will almost certainly pick up within the exposure.

Screen and stencil orientation

You also need to find the best orientation for the stencils on your screen prior to exposure. If you have a portrait stencil, for example, it's best to expose it in the portrait aspect on the screen so you are printing the narrow edge. You need to allow at least 10–12cm at both the top and the bottom of the screen as there needs to be room for the ink in between pulls, as well as room at the bottom of the screen to maintain a 45-degree angle to cover the image.

Ensure that you leave plenty of space around the edge of the stencil to accommodate the squeegee and ink. There should be at least a 5cm border between the stencil and the edges of the screen otherwise you will find it difficult to print the stencil. The mesh is also very tight in this area and can easily split.

Calculating exposure times

Exposure depends on the power of the UV light source and the distance to the screen placed on the glass. The mesh count can also make a difference. A coarse mesh such as T45 will hold more emulsion and therefore create a thicker stencil, which will take longer to expose. The stencil material will also make a difference. If the stencils have been made from tracing paper the light will take longer to break through, whereas clear acetate will require a much shorter exposure.

It can be difficult to work out the time for different materials and screens. An exposure calculator can be used effectively when you are just getting started. As you progress you will have a rough idea of what times to use.

An exposure calculator is a piece of printed acetate with five identical columns combined with five different filters. Each filter cuts down the amount of light that can penetrate the screen by a factor of –0.25.

To use the calculator, take a guess at the exposure and double it. Expose the screen and wash out. There should be a gradual colour change across the columns from dark to light. The column where the change stops has the ideal exposure. Read the number at the top of the column and multiply by the exposure. This will give you the correct exposure.

For example, if you use an exposure time of 6 minutes, double this time and expose the screen for 12 minutes. Refer to the calculator when you have exposed the screen.

If the ideal exposure indicates a factor of 0.7, multiply this by 12 (0.7 × 12) to give a total of 8.4 minutes.

Placing stencils on top of exposure unit

Place your stencil or stencils on top of the exposure unit glass, so that they face the right way round. Take into consideration the orientation as discussed above. The UV light source will expose everything that sits within the box edge.

EQUIPMENT AND MATERIALS

* Screen (90 mesh count) coated with photo emulsion
* Exposure box and UV light
* Access to a shower spray or hosepipe
* Exposure calculator (optional)
* Transparency with design

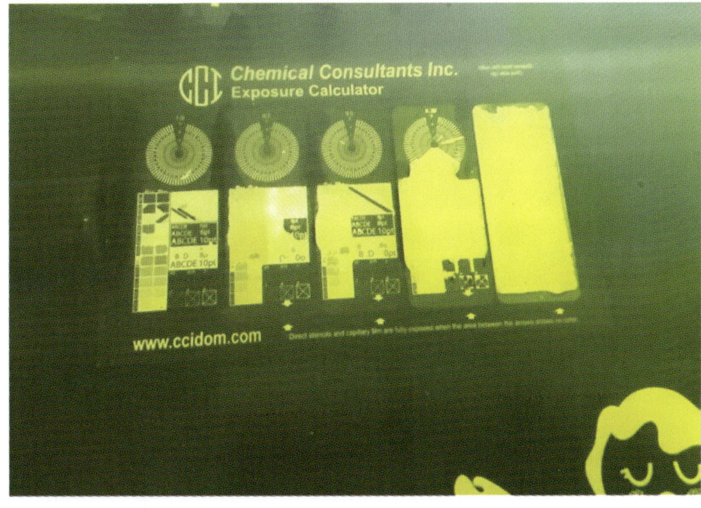

Typical exposure calculator.

Two stencils are placed on the glass side by side, facing the right way around.

The screen is positioned over the stencils ensuring a gap on both sides of the images.

Heavy books make good weights to keep the screen in full contact with the stencil images.

Place the back of screen on top of the stencil

Carefully place the prepared screen on top of the stencil and glass, checking that the stencils haven't moved on the glass. You may notice a small gap between the stencils and screen, and you need to make sure that this gap is closed as much as possible.

Ensure good contact between stencil and screen

Place the cutting board or a sheet of heavy rubber inside the screen and on top of the glass and stencil to reduce the gap and get a good fit between the stencil and screen. Placing a few heavy objects on top of the board will weigh it down even further.

Cover and expose the screen

Complete the set-up with a cover or blanket before making the exposure. The average exposure time should be about 6 minutes. Remove the screen from the top of the exposure unit and make sure that you put the transparency in a safe place as you will need it later.

Develop the screen in cold water

Using a shower head, spray water on both sides of the screen. Be consistent when you are washing away the emulsion by moving the shower head across the screen from top to bottom. The emulsion will slowly start to wash away in a blue flow, gradually reducing in colour and revealing the exposed image. The areas that have washed away are the printable areas: the blue emulsion that is left on the screen will resist the ink. Spray water evenly across the emulsion as you need to remove all the unexposed emulsion. If any emulsion is left on the screen it can run into the stencil areas of the screen and block them.

Leave the screen to dry

The screen stencil is still soft at this stage, so be careful not to mark it with your hands. Leave the screen to dry completely. This doesn't need to be in the dark. Dry the screen in a dust-free environment. Depending on the temperature you may have to wait overnight to print, but the screen-drying process can be sped up using a fan heater.

Cover any pinholes with screen filler

Any areas that you don't want to print, such as particles of dust and pinholes, can be covered over using filler on the back of the screen. Don't be tempted to paint large quantities of filler on the screen. You just need to fill the holes. The filler should also be removed at the end of printing.

Tape the well of the screen

Use good-quality masking tape to mask between the edge of the screen and the frame, taping the well of the screen inside so that it overlaps the stencil. You don't want any ink to creep under the edge of the screen. Masking the frame makes cleaning up much easier too and protects the screen against ink build-up.

Adjusting the snap

As described in Chapter 2 there should be a small gap between the screen and the paper to prevent the paper sticking to the screen. Remember to attach a couple of pieces of card to the front of the screen to create and adjust the snap. If one side of the print is still sticking to the screen raise the snap.

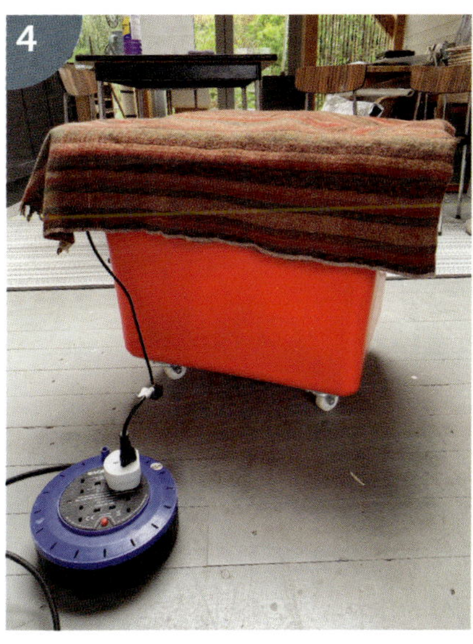

Cover all sides of the exposure unit to limit the escape of UV light.

The screen can be developed outside if it is a cloudy day. Make sure you apply a spray of water as soon as possible.

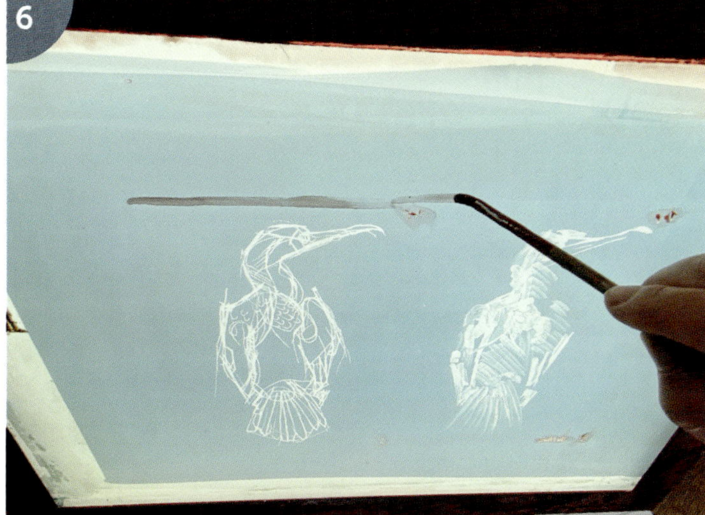

Paint out any pinholes with filler on the back of the screen.

Use strong paper tape to mask the inside of screens.

TROUBLESHOOTING – STENCIL EXPOSURE

Stencil washing off screen

This means that either the exposure has been too short or the emulsion has been coated too thickly or uneven. Refer to your exposure guide or try increasing the exposure. It could also indicate that the emulsion is out of date.

Loss of detail in the exposed stencil

This is usually due to a thin positive that is not very lightproof. You will need to darken the positive by hand or increase the tone if printing digitally. You can also try reducing the exposure time, but this might result in a very thin stencil.

REGISTERING PHOTO STENCILS

Registering your prints so they align with subsequent printed layers is a delicate art and it can be frustrating if you have several colours that are all slightly out of position. Take care to ensure that the screens are tightly attached to the clamps and the screens can't move about, as this can

The second colour has been masked out on the screen using a piece of acetate. This will prevent ink seeping through the stencil and keep the screen clean in these areas during printing.

Mix a light and dark colour range.

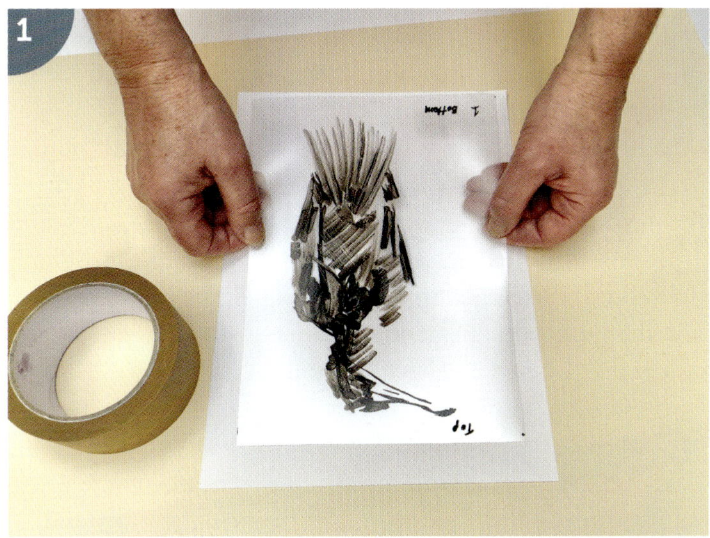

Step 1. Place the first stencil where you want it to print on the paper and tape in position

Step 2. Position stencil underneath the screen

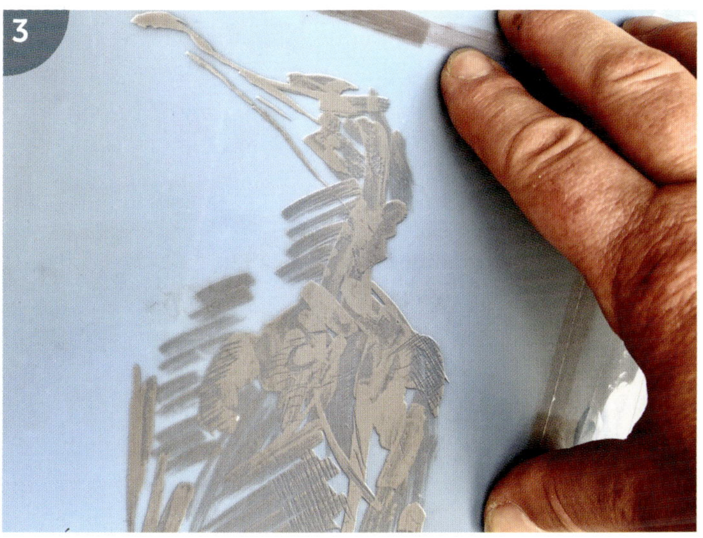

Step 3. Match up the stencil with the screen image

Step 4. Tape the stencil in position and add the registration stops

result in a great deal of misregistration throughout the printing process.

Make sure that the paper is cut accurately. If you are using paper registration stops, take care that each print is placed in the correct position. Don't rush this process.

After you have masked the screen, attach it to the printing baseboard using the same screen clamps. Mix ink as required ready to print.

There are two different methods of registering your print:

Method 1: Registration stops

This method was covered in Chapter 2 and uses small registration stops on the baseboard into which the printing paper is fitted prior to printing.

There are several methods of matching up the screen stencil with the printing paper. I attach the acetate stencil on the printing paper where I want it to print, then place it under the screen and match it with the screen stencil.

There is an art to matching up the two images. Everything might be in position and then a slight movement on the table makes everything shift. Try attaching card extensions to your paper and move the paper around with the screen in the down position.

When both stencils match, quickly tape the stencil and paper on the baseboard and add the registration stops in the normal way.

Beware this method is not always print foolproof. When the screen is stretched to meet the paper, the image may not line up as you imagined. Where registration may be an issue I use the acetate sheet method.

Method 2: Registration using an acetate copy

This method is great with multicoloured prints where you want to ensure that the top colours fit over those printed below. A sheet of acetate (Maylar) is attached to the bottom of the baseboard using a taped hinge. The image is printed on the acetate. The paper with the other printed layer is slid underneath and matched up. The acetate sheet is then removed and printing resumed.

You need to do this for each print, but you can still use registration stops to position prints as closely as possible.

Simply attach a piece of Mylar film to the edge of the baseboard on the left-hand side. Make sure it is big enough to cover the printing area. Tape it down with masking tape so it can flip/hinge over on top of the printing area.

After printing the top colour on the acetate sheet, the first printed layer was placed underneath and aligned with the top design.

Remove the Mylar by flipping it away from the printing table and print. Repeat this process.

PRINTING PHOTO STENCILS

Printing from photo silkscreens is a relatively easy process because the designs are flush and embedded in the screen mesh. It is also easier to print long runs and you can clean the screen and store it for later use. A screen I use for demonstration purposes has been going strong for more than five years. You must be sure, however, to remove all ink residue after use on both sides with a hose and sponge before drying and storage.

Because the image is flush with the mesh the amount of ink laid down on the paper is relatively thin. If you want to increase the opacity simply give the stencil a second pull and it will dramatically darken the tone.

When the paper is registered you can start to print the first colour. Try mixing ink on the screen.

Hang the prints to dry, but be careful to keep them apart.

After printing, scrape any ink off the screen with a palette knife. Clean the screen on both sides with warm water and a microfibre cloth and dry before covering the first printed image with acetate or paper.

Place the second stencil over one of the dry prints and match the images. Secure with tape.

Register the second stencil on the baseboard through the screen as before and add the registration stops.

Print the top colour and hang the prints to dry. Clean the screen as before.

REMOVING PHOTO EMULSION AND RECLAIMING THE SILKSCREEN

After removing ink and protective tapes, screens should be cleaned with water immediately after printing on both sides. This can be done in situ. Stripping the exposed photo stencil from the screen requires a specific emulsion remover. You will need protective clothing including gloves, a facemask and goggles.

Method

The usual way is to dilute the emulsion remover with water and apply it to both sides of the dry screen with a bristle brush, working it into the mesh. Leave it to soak for a few minutes and repeat the process. You will start to notice the stencil and emulsion breaking down on the mesh and runing away off the screen. Keep rubbing the remover into the mesh and make sure you cover all areas of the screen and frame.

When you are confident that the stencil has broken down enough, use a hosepipe or power washer to clean the screen on both sides, including the frame. Make sure you remove all of the stencil and acrylic ink; stains can build up over time making your screens useless.

Finally degrease the screen and leave it to dry.

If possible, emulsion should be removed from the screen outdoors. Use a hose and make sure you flush the water down a drain.

EQUIPMENT AND MATERIALS

* Screen cleaning brush
* Power washer or hosepipe
* Photo emulsion remover/de-coater solution
* Screen degreasing solution

TROUBLESHOOTING – PHOTO STENCIL PRINT

Ink drying in the mesh

Ink drying in the mesh can be a problem, particularly if you have a lot of fine detail or if you are at the end of a long run and your ink has thickened on the screen. This can be overcome by working quickly and making sure that you add a few drops of retarder to the ink before printing. All being well this will stop the ink from drying in the mesh and give you plenty of time to finish the print run.

Blocked areas of the stencil

Fine detail can be easily blocked on a small screen during a run, particularly if you are working on your own. Clean the area with a microfibre cloth both back and front with clean water. Do not soak the screen and do not remove any other ink. Flood the screen and print on newsprint to clear the area before resuming printing.

Pinholes are leaking ink

Filler can leak ink particularly towards the end of a print run. Tape holes with Sellotape on the underside of the screen.

Lines appearing in the print

This could be due to a nick in the squeegee, or there may be some debris in the ink. Turn the squeegee round and use the other side of the blade. Remove the ink, clean the screen and start again.

PHOTO SILKSCREEN: SIMPLE ANALOGUE STENCILS

In this section I have listed a variety of transparent materials suitable for painting and drawing. These materials are excellent for creating photo stencils due to their distinct properties. Additionally, numerous drawing and painting mediums are available for experimentation, and it is likely that you will discover new ones to add to this compilation.

The stencil-making process necessitates designs that are 'positive' or oriented correctly. These designs can be produced using an inkjet or laser printer on clear acetate sheets or can be hand-painted directly onto transparent films such as cellophane.

Before beginning your experiments with photo silkscreen, it is advisable to invest in an LED light box that is adequately sized for your screens. This tool is invaluable for composing designs and addressing any pinholes on your screens. By placing the design on top of the light box and securing the stencil film over it, the LED illumination will facilitate the transfer of designs onto the film, ensuring the desired opacity. It also allows for meticulous mark-making by making scratches visible.

Furthermore, it is essential to consider the screen size, screen mesh and paper before commencing. Ensure that your design fits comfortably on the screen with ample margins and that the mesh is sufficiently fine to capture all the intricate details of your creation.

Choosing the right transparent surface for stencils

Selecting the right transparent surface to make your stencils depends on the artwork you are creating and your attitude to design and mark-making. Silkscreen has

Florists' acetate is an inexpensive and great surface to paint on.

True-Grain picks up textural and tonal detail in the grainy surface.

been transformed in recent years by the introduction of new drawing and painting films that can pick up lovely textured marks and tonal details. I have listed a few of my favourites below:

Florists' acetate

I generally use florists' acetate to create my artwork as it's cheap. I like painting on the surface with Indian ink as you can smudge the ink and scratch into the surface, adding depth to the design when it's dry. Go for the thickest acetate you can buy.

True-Grain and Mark Resist film

Other surfaces that you can use are more technical and made for the professional printer. These include True-Grain, which reproduces fine, medium and dark tones using wet and dry materials. The surface has a fine texture that picks up detail on the surface that reproduces like a lithographic print. The downside is that the film is very expensive. A very similar alternative, but much cheaper, is Mark Resist film.

Mylar

Mylar film is another popular choice among printmakers for stencil making. It is a type of polyester film that is highly durable and resistant to tearing. Mylar's smooth, non-porous surface ensures that paint and ink do not seep through, providing crisp and clean stencil edges. I use sheets in 125 microns. It is also easy to paint and draw on with both ink and acrylic ink. I also use Mylar to register my multicoloured prints as it is easy to clean and reuse. To make your own film that can pick up tonal variations, I lightly sand the surface of the film to create a textured surface to paint on.

Tracing paper

I have used tracing paper quite successfully to make stencils for silkscreen, although it does not take wet media very well. I prefer to use it for tonal drawings. If I am going to paint it, I generally use black acrylic.

Transparent photocopy

It is also easy to photocopy or output a design via an inkjet or laser printer. Make sure you buy the appropriate printing film. Use the printer's settings to accept transparencies and print the image in black and white on a high resolution.

Maylar has a super smooth surface, and marks can easily be removed with methylated spirits.

Tracing paper can be used with dry and wet media and is good at capturing tone.

Creating effective stencils for printmaking

Hand-painted stencils offer a unique and personal touch to printmaking. To achieve the best results, however, it is essential to use a paint or ink capable of effectively blocking out light. This is crucial in ensuring that the design remains clear and impenetrable to light.

When it comes to choosing the right paint or ink for your stencils, high-quality Indian ink or black acrylic paint are excellent choices. These materials are dense and opaque enough to block out light completely. While it might be tempting to experiment with coloured paints, remember that the primary goal is to create a stencil that is impenetrable to light. Coloured paints often lack the opacity necessary to achieve this, leading to less effective results.

Before applying ink or paint, ensure that the stencil surface is clean and free of dust or debris. This will help the ink or paint adhere better and create a smoother finish.

Please note that your stencils should be completely dry before putting them on the exposure unit or brought into contact with the screen emulsion.

If you are printing multicoloured designs, you need to break the colours down into separate stencils and print any under-colours first. The next chapter deals with this in more detail.

Indian ink

This expressive ink can be painted on most transparent surfaces. If you add methylated spirits or turpentine you can produce some lovely dispersal tones and marks.

Acrylic paint

This has more body than the ink, so it can be controlled more easily. It does, however, dry quickly and can be scratched. It is easy to create tones. The paint can be mixed with water, but you should avoid dilution or you will create a thin stencil.

Water-based wax crayons

When used on a textured surface such as True-Grain you can't beat these crayons for hand-drawn marks. Only use a black crayon and add water to produce tonal values or scratch to remove areas and add more texture.

Acrylic paint pens

These come in different sizes and are expensive. They are very opaque, so they can be used to draw lines on surfaces such as acetate and tracing paper.

Ink pens

Try traditional dip pens and Indian ink for scratchy, inky lines.

Paper stencils

Try cutting paper stencils and spraying with black paint. Alternatively stencils cut from black paper make very effective photo stencils and give a handmade appearance.

Textural rubbings

These can be made by placing the textured material underneath the surface of the stencil film. Water-based wax crayons work well and can be washed away, scratched or diluted with water to create a painterly effect.

Linocut and collagraph stencils

Ink up your linocuts and collagraphs with a water-based relief printing ink. It is a good idea to sand the surface of the print block first, which helps the ink to adhere to the surface. Apply a transparent sheet over the top of the printing plate and print onto the plastic sheet. You can use the design on either side of the transparent sheet.

You can copy your artwork straight from a sketchbook onto film, making it easy to create a transparency for photo silkscreen – as long as your image is dark enough for the process.

TROUBLESHOOTING – PHOTO SILKSCREEN

Photo emulsion unexposed

Note that unexposed emulsion can be washed off the screen without any special cleaner. If you make a mistake that can't be rectified, simply shower the emulsion off the screen, degrease and start again.

Emulsion too thick

You can remove excess emulsion by pulling the trough back up the screen. This can be done without adding any more emulsion to the screen.

Uneven photo emulsion application

There is not enough emulsion in the trough or it is not evenly distributed. Make sure that the trough has evenly distributed emulsion in the gutter. When you tip the trough up, wait for all the emulsion to drip down onto the leading edge evenly.

Areas of screen that have resisted the emulsion

This is caused by greasy marks or dust on the screen. You will need to degrease the screen, dry and start again. Dusty or greasy screens can cause lots of problems after the emulsion is dry as you need to fill all the pinholes that occur.

The design hasn't appeared when the screen is washed out

You have overexposed the screen, or the stencil is not opaque enough. Try reducing the exposure time or darkening the stencil.

The background emulsion has started to come off the screen and become very thin

The main reason for this is underexposure, so you may need to increase the exposure time. Other reasons may be that you have used an overly powerful hose to clean away the emulsion or had the spray too close to the screen.

The design detail has filled in

There are several reasons why this could be the case, including overexposure and too low a mesh count. Try increasing the mesh count or reducing the exposure time.

CHAPTER 6

IMAGE DESIGN AND STENCIL MAKING FOR PHOTO SILKSCREEN PRINTING

You will quickly develop a way of translating your creative designs into silkscreen prints and if you get bitten by the process you will start to build your own individual approach. It's important to keep trying new ways of working and keeping your work fresh and exciting. As already discussed, there are lots of different methods of making photo stencils and the previous chapter introduced you to materials and methods you can use to make hand-painted and drawn stencils.

In this chapter we will explore in more detail different approaches to analogue design and ways of preparing and making artwork that captures painted tone and texture. I will discuss a range of design formats and how to combine different stencil techniques. There is also a detailed description of how to register multicoloured stencils and print a small edition.

I will use some of my own prints as examples to illustrate different printing methods and unpack the process behind their creation. There are also a couple of project briefs that combine different media, which should give you a flavour of how easy it is to combine hand-painted stencils and black-and-white paper artwork.

'Apple Season' incorporates photo and hand-cut stencils.

Detail from 'Last Flight', a multi-stencil print combining silhouettes and hand-painted collage.

GETTING STARTED: DESIGN IN MIND

Design is a necessary part of the print process. You may want to tell a story, describe a plant or animal, or get a message across. Equally your main motive could be to convey a mood or feeling. Everyone goes about the design process in a distinctive way.

The following design considerations are aimed at getting you to think about where you feel comfortable within the design process and offer an insight into some basic visual elements and tips that I use when developing my designs. Feel free to challenge yourself and experiment. If you don't generally pick up a paintbrush, take the plunge and give it a go. If texture is not your thing – make it a prominent feature.

Design inspiration

I use my sketchbooks as my initial jumping off point. They reflect my interest in the environment and my drawing skills, which I try to capture in my prints. I don't always start with a plan as my sketchbook drawings are part of my day-to-day life and a record of whatever has piqued my curiosity. I may start a print and have a visual in mind, but my imagination may take the idea in an entirely different direction. I do, however, enjoy narrative and there is always a story behind my printmaking. This could be a reference

Sketchbook inspiration for 'The Grape Pickers'.

to a seasonal activity in the garden, a collection of favourite objects that I have simplified, or a combination of drawn objects in an imaginative landscape.

Design process

Starting with a design and purpose in mind is useful, but it is not essential as you might prefer an organic approach where you respond to how a print is developing. For example, combining different printing techniques may have an impact on how the finished result develops. If you have a specific purpose in mind, however, such as a double-sided card, poster or small print, a considered design approach may be more applicable.

Before you begin making your photo stencils you need to consider print size, paper and screen format, what transparent material you are going to use to make the stencils and what kind of marks you want to make. For example, you may want to print some textures in advance and collage them onto your design film or photocopy some photographs.

Consider how experimental you're going to be as well and try out some ideas first before embarking on a large print run. You may find, for example, that colour combinations do not always work as you expected, and you may not be able to pick up as much detail from the photo stencil and may need to change the exposure.

Print size and printing area

Before you begin your design, specify the size and shape of the printing area and work within these parameters. It's easy to get distracted and expand the design beyond your printing capabilities.

Using paper in standard 'A' sizes results in some restrictions in terms of layout and design fit. Try to consider other print shapes as well as screen masks if you are going to combine monoprint with photo silkscreen. I often use square proportions, which are also easy to mask out by hand.

The size of prints will be determined by both screen size and the size of your exposure box. You will also need to plan for a border so that you can easily handle and dry the prints. I suggest that you maintain an A4/A3 format or similar when starting to experiment as this will ensure that your designs fit on most available printing paper.

Consider how much paper might be wasted too if you need to trim standard paper size, for example if printing a square format on rectangular-shaped paper.

Stencil material should be cut to fit within the paper size where possible. You should also plan a simple print strategy in a notebook, recording print details such as colours, stencil materials, size, paper and layout. Recording the process and outcome will enable you to assess what worked and where you can make improvements.

Using templates to create designs

When I start my design compositions I always refer to my original drawings and make small-scale, coloured design sketches. I explore landscape, portrait and square reworkings to determine what format works for my design.

When I have a sense of what structures I want to include in my design I pull elements from my sketchbook, which I quickly redraw on a sheet of newsprint maintaining the size of the finished print. I often make paper templates of images that I can reorganise and move within the design space before sticking them lightly in position. I redraw my final composition on newsprint in a soft black pencil or charcoal and label the printed layers. I keep these drawings loose and add tonal variations.

Design components

Visual energy and tensions

When you are translating your ideas from a sketchbook to a design layout consider how individual elements react with one another to create energies and tensions. How can you grab attention, create curiosity or capture movement. Consider the forces that lines, shapes and colours can exert across the design space.

I use loose, spontaneous marks and gestures that suggest energy when creating my artwork. I also use contrasting and complementary colours to make some elements more prominent. I work quickly and often time myself to avoid overworking.

Colour

Colour is the most affecting of all design components. It stimulates the viewer's feelings and adds harmony to a design. Not everyone sees colour in the same way, however, so it is important that you do not rely on colour alone within the design. Consider using one dominant hue and then adding other shades of the same colour as under-colours.

Balance

Keep the design balanced and think about the contrast between elements. Contrast comes in lots of different forms, such as placing a rough texture next to a linear illustration or a bright colour next to a darker tone. Contrast also creates visual interest and attracts the viewer.

White space and overlapping

Consider the white space or areas that don't contain any print. These are just as important. Don't be afraid to overlap elements to create new viewpoints.

Focal points

Focal points are the areas in your work to which the eye is first drawn. They have the greatest dominance and gain the attention of the viewer's eye first before exploring the rest of the design. Try creating designs with different focal emphasis, for example placing it just off-centre or on the outside edge of the printing shape. The design can also have different points of interest and can be determined by contrast of shape, colour, scale, texture and so on.

Designing with templates enables you to move different parts of the design around the design space before settling on an arrangement.

PHOTO STENCILS: ACETATE COLLAGE

Stencils that are made from collaged acetate elements can give your prints a three-dimensional impact. Acetates can have a range of solid and transparent areas and can be very effective when printed, revealing under-colours and interacting with the layers beneath.

Stencils are constructed like a paper collage, only using pieces of decorated film that you can either make in advance or simply reuse. I keep a bag of acetate bits for this purpose and cut and re-form them to fit my designs. This method of reworking ensures unplanned use of surfaces and underlays.

As already mentioned, thumbnail sketches are a good way of moving ideas out of a sketchbook and onto a page where you can develop elements such as structure and colour.

A paper design collage can be created to size on thin paper and moved around the design space. Once you have settled on a design and considered colour fills you can go about making the necessary design layers for a multilayered photo stencil print.

EQUIPMENT AND MATERIALS

Printing

* All silkscreen printing materials and equipment including three–four screens coated with emulsion
* Printing paper
* Printing ink (three–four colours mixed)

Design and Stencil Making

* Newsprint
* Drawing materials
* Lightbox (optional)
* Stencil film – Maylar, cellophane etc; 4 sheets cut to size (A4/A3)
* Film for collage
* Craft knife and cutting board
* Scissors
* Mark-making materials: Indian ink, wax crayons, acrylic paint etc
* Glue stick or spray glue
* Paint brushes
* Masking tape

Sketchbook paintings can provide inspiration, generating ideas for print structure and colour.

Method

I suggest working within an A3 or A4 size and three or four print layers. Resize your design on a sheet of newsprint and employ some of the design methods suggested overleaf. Each layer or colour will be created by making a separate stencil that is drawn or painted on stencil film or cut out of existing stencil material. Each colour is collaged on a separate piece of acetate and stuck in position.

The stencil layers are assembled in print order. The paler colours are printed first and are covered by the darker top colours.

Make sure that you have a design to work from and have outlined the size. It should be the right size for the printing

Central orientation
Utilising the centre of the design space is a powerful placement. It is not essential to place the element right in the centre of the page. You could make it the largest component and, in this example, place it on a textured base at the bottom of the page.

Just off centre
This is a popular placement as it still grabs attention but is in a secure location in relation to the other elements that occupy central locations. It unifies the shape of the design and, as it doesn't occupy the centre, enables the viewer to see the detail in the foreground.

Elements at the bottom of the design
Elements that are placed at the bottom of a design are more grounded and less active within a composition. The leaf shape at the bottom of this print grabs all the attention.

Objects placed high up in a design
These are more active and dynamic. They carry more weight the further away from the centre they are. Large typographical headings are a good example of grabbing all the attention.

Left and right outside edge orientation
Elements that engage with the outside edge, as in this design, develop a very powerful position. Where two or more elements share the edge, however, neither is as prominent as if it had the edge to itself. Simple use of complementary colours and the positioning of the dark silhouette shapes restore balance.

Grid
Designing within an underlying grid provides a framework to align your elements and helps to create harmonious configurations. Although a grid consists of columns and rows how these are spaced and divided is in response to the content that is held within their section. Grids also provide a great opportunity for colour relations and moving colour around in a design.

Symmetrical arrangements
Symmetrical design arrangements are generally compositions that use mirror images along a central axis to create a balanced design and are the same on both sides. I prefer to create visual tension by using very similar elements with some variations on both sides. This print uses the same chair element but contains a range of different textures and variations across the print.

Asymmetrical arrangements
Establishing a balanced design without the use of mirrored elements around a central placement requires design parts that offset one another equally. Asymmetry has no firm rules. In this example the large swirl on the left is balanced by the smaller leaves and line structures creating an overall feeling of balance. Intense colours are also balanced by neutrals.

Repetition and rhythm
These qualities go hand in hand in design terms and bring unity to a design. My print 'Shoal' uses overlapping fish silhouettes, but each has a unique body decoration with contrasting colours. Employing a regular and repeating sequence of elements suggests movement in a pattern or design. You can express rhythm by simply repeating a design or motif across the print area.

Lines
Lines are a major part of my creative practice as I love drawing, but many find them a struggle to control. Lines can be used printed on top of blocks of colour, used to create depths of shade, or emphasise a shape and bring it forward in the design.

paper and can be accommodated by the screens. Decide what and how many colours you want to print and how they will fit together within the design.

Stencil making: Making colour separations

When making the stencils think about mark-making and what kind of materials you want to use to create these. Do you want to create painterly texture or hand-drawn effects? Refer to the stencil materials listed in Chapter 5 to decide what materials and film work best for you.

You can create a selection of textures using such means as rubbing techniques and paint splattering and cut them to create your design. You can work into these textures afterwards by scratching with a scissor point.

Each colour will require a separate transparency or 'positive'. Start by labelling these with the colour choice and orientation, such as top and bottom of the design. This will also help when the stencils are exposed and ensure that you get them the right way round. This text can be included in the photo stencil and will be blocked out during the printing.

In this example a background window and decorative floor were made from textured rubbings using a black wax crayon and cut to shape with a pair of scissors before collaging into position with a glue stick.

A simple paper cartoon contains all the basic design elements and is drawn on newsprint and pasted into position.

Painted design elements are cut out of acetate sheets and moved around the design area.

The detailed pots were hand-drawn on acetate using an acrylic pen and cut and collaged. White outlines were introduced by removing ink with a craft knife.

A background plant silhouette positioned on top of the window was printed in a mid-tone, painted with Indian ink and acrylic pens. The main plant design was painted on cellophane with Indian ink. The design was scratched after drying to create texture.

Ink choice

This print used five colours: two or three light under-colours and two darker textural colours on top. Remember that the white of the paper is also a colour and can be used to great effect in a design. You can also mix ink on the screen during the printing process to create colour variations.

Always test your colours before you print by masking a screen and dragging a line of colour across, or by simply dragging colour across the paper with a squeegee. Determine how the colours interact with one another. This print uses dark, medium and light tones. Make sure that you use the paper you are going to print on to assess the tone. Handmade papers will absorb more colour than smooth papers.

All stencils are aligned on top of one another on the printing paper in printing order to ensure that they fit. Here stencil 1 is at the bottom and stencil 5 on the top.

Stencil exposure

Make a photo stencil of each transparency. If you can accommodate more than one colour on a screen, this will help with resources and cleaning.

You may need to experiment with exposure times to capture some of the textures that you have made on the stencils.

Registration and printing

As this is a multicoloured stencil, the Maylar method of registration was used. Registration stops were also added.

Tape a sheet of Maylar at the bottom of the printing baseboard, large enough to cover the printing area. Use a strong plastic tape and ensure that you can move the film in and out of position.

Create a vibrant colour scheme from pale through to dark colours.

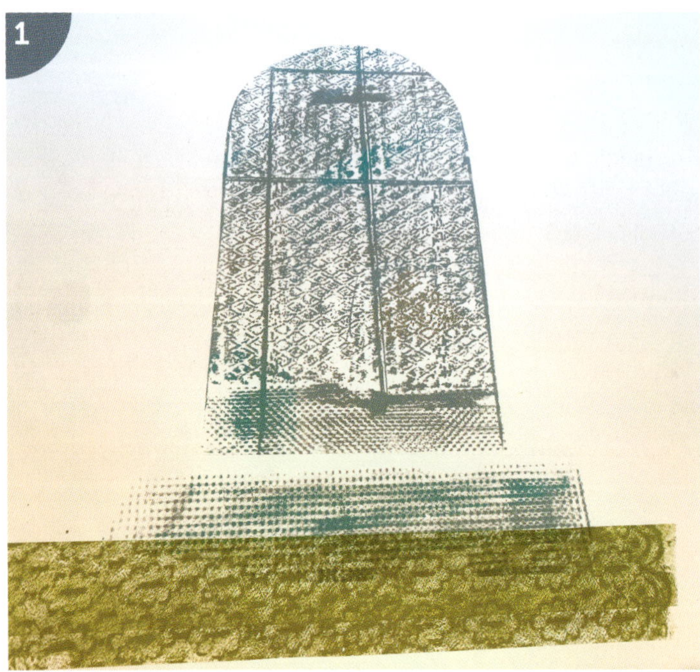

Start to build the background colours that sit behind the main design detail. The olive green decorative strip was printed on top of the grey window.

Place the third stencil on top of the first colour, align and tape in position.

Print the mid-tones. Coloured inks can be mixed on the screen using swift movements with a palette knife to create a range of new tones. Notice the colour mixing and blending on the plant silhouettes providing more interest.

The dark green detail was added.

PHOTO STENCILS: PAPER ARTWORK TO DIGITAL STENCIL

This is a really simple way of making stencils for photo silkscreen and uses basic digital technology and handmade artwork. Any flat artwork including magazine or newspaper collage can be used as well as the likes of sketchbook drawings and photographs. It is not essential but helps if you are working in black and white. You can also combine collaged film as well as decorated papers together.

'Pot and Prune', a collaged paper-stencil print combining hand-drawn and painted elements.

EQUIPMENT AND MATERIALS

You will need access to a device to scan your artwork and a digital printer to make the stencil.

* Scalpel and cutting board
* Scissors
* Light box
* Glue stick
* White mount board
* Black fine liners, acrylic pens, Indian ink etc.
* Photocopy acetate
* Acetate for making background stencils

Method

Simply copy a hand-drawn or collaged design by either taking a photograph on a mobile phone or by scanning the image in to a computer. Digitally created artwork using programs such as Adobe Illustrator or Photoshop employs vector graphics, which give clean, scalable pictures regardless of how much you scale them up or down. A photo or scanned artwork, however, is stored as a raster file, such as a JPEG, PNG and GIF. These files are also referred to as bitmaps as they convert the design into dots or pixels. Depending on the resolution of these dots, the edges of the design can become blurred when enlarged.

I regularly scan or photograph hand-drawn artwork at 600dpi, the highest resolution I have available on my scanner and camera, and output this in black and white on a transparency.

Bear in mind that once you have copied your design you can scale it up or down, but remember that if you make it larger than the original artwork the edges may become blurred.

Creating the artwork

I make drawings or paintings on paper with a black-and-white fine liner or Indian ink. I also photocopy my sketchbook drawings and paintings and incorporate these in my designs.

By cutting and pasting design elements into position on a piece of white mounting board it is possible to collage lots of paper textures too. My print 'Pot and Prune' is a good example of a photocopied stencil combined with two hand-drawn stencils to add colour across the central area of the design.

This design started life as lots of small sketches of my greenhouse and surrounding orchard. I decided that the overall design would be a simple outline drawing containing some collaged elements. Notice the use of newspaper print and decorated paper in the plant forms. I wanted to convey outdoor and indoor gardening activities without drawing every panel of glass in the greenhouse. I decided to keep the design looking as handmade as possible.

I started with an A3 landscape format and created the different illustrations using a combination of black ink pen drawings, which I made on lightweight paper, and cut paper collage. I played around with the design for a while, mixing photocopied textures and my own painted outlines. When I was happy with the design, I glued everything down with spray glue.

The hand-drawn artwork was scanned on my computer scanner at 600dpi and the resulting JPEG was printed in black and white on acetate using a copy shop photocopier.

Adding hand-painted stencils

The print has a simple colour scheme. Two hand-painted stencils sit behind the drawn elements and were printed in pale green and yellow. These were painted on florists' acetate and texture was scratched into them when they were dry.

I made photo stencils of all the colours and experimented with different colour variations. I didn't want the background colours to overpower the delicate lines and textures of the collaged work, so kept the palette simple.

Print registration

To register the print, I positioned the black stencil where needed on the printing paper and taped it in position. Then, aligning the olive-green stencil beneath it, I secured it and removed the black stencil.

The black top stencil was removed. The olive-green screen was fixed to the board and aligned through the mesh for printing. This process was repeated for the pale-yellow under colour, finishing with the black print using the Maylar method.

Collaged elements in 'Pot and Prune' include newspaper print, handmade textures cut from white paper and black-and-white magazine photos.

PROJECT: CREATING A TWO-COLOUR PHOTO SILKSCREEN PRINT

This project will create a simple two-coloured print from paper artwork and a hand-painted stencil. You can use an existing sketchbook drawing, a collage or perhaps make something new.

Method

For this you should use an A5 or A4 format and choose a simple open design in which an under-colour will show through a top detailed image. The detailed image will be photocopied and the under-colour will be made from a hand-painted stencil.

Consider how other textures can be added through collage to the main design. If you are using an existing drawing, this can be photocopied and the design can be enlarged or reduced, with textures pasted into it.

EQUIPMENT AND MATERIALS

As well as the equipment and materials listed you will need access to a mobile phone, a black-and-white home printer and local copy shop that can print on acetate. You also might be able to print on acetate on your inkjet printer.

Printing Equipment

* Two screens and baseboard
* Squeegee
* Photo stencil equipment and materials
* Palette knives
* Printing inks (two colours)

Design Materials and equipment

* Printing paper
* Masking tape
* Maylar (for registration)
* Printing acetate (A4/A3)
* Sketchbook drawing or collage papers
* Drawing materials
* White paper or card
* Scalpel and cutting board
* Glue stick
* Black liners, Indian ink

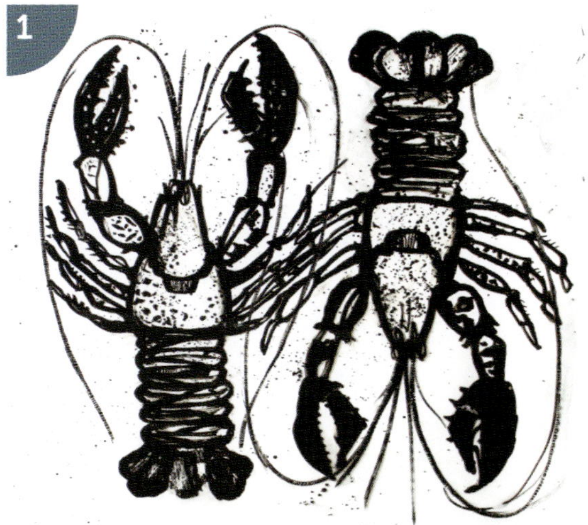

1 Construct your top design on a white piece of film paper or card in black and white only.

2 This design is photographed with a phone in good light.

3 The photo is sent directly to an inkjet printer to print on A4 acetate.

Using Indian ink, an under-colour stencil is painted on acetate to fit beneath the top design.

Photo stencils are made of both colours. The under-colour (orange) is printed first.

The top black detail brings the design together.

PAINTED PHOTO STENCILS AND PAPER-STENCIL COMBINATION

I like to get a lot of colours into my prints without making numerous photo stencils. This is done by blending colours into one another on the screen. I also like to combine paper stencils with photo stencils as they are particularly good at covering large areas. You can also move the paper about on the screen to get different print variations.

My print 'The Grape Pickers' combines two photo stencils on two separate screens with a multi-paper stencil montage. The design originated in my sketchbook. Although I liked the simplicity of the blue and white in the original, I decided to go for a 'moody' colour scheme that highlighted the figures with their baskets of red fruit. I scaled the drawing to A2 on a sheet of newsprint.

I also considered how to print the background. I didn't want a regular straight rectangle as I was trying to replicate my hand-drawn sketchbook marks, but I wanted the print to sit on a coloured background. The solution was to recreate a painted photo stencil background on an acetate sheet that captured brushmarks and texture.

Method

Both stencils were hand-painted on florists' acetate using Indian ink. The photo stencil background was also painted with Indian ink. The top stencil was painted quickly, using lots of different mark-making materials, including feathers and thin ink pens.

The paper stencils took most of the time. I cut out lots of shapes, masking out the highlights of the figures and the peacock and tearing random ribbon shapes. All the paper stencils were created from newspaper.

Artist Zoë Eaddy's print combines a hand-painted photo stencil and a series of hand-cut paper stencils.

This stencil was hand-painted on florists' acetate using Indian ink.

Ink choice

I made a photo stencil of the top design and printed four copies on white cartridge paper. I then mixed up a broad range of colours, using greens and reds in pale and medium shades, and painted over the printed design. I made different variations and then chose a colour palette that worked best.

Printing the paper-stencil background

Using the background screen and working from light to dark, I masked out the design areas with paper stencils and printed different layers on top of one another, maintaining the highlights behind the figures and red fruit baskets. I also printed a white layer on the edge of the fruit to knock the colour back.

The background consisted of three layers. I removed the stencils and cleaned the screens in-between colours. The screen and registration stops remained in situ throughout. The finished background has a nice combination of hand-cut and torn paper-stencil shapes.

Printing the top stencil

The screen mask was replaced by the top photo stencil in the printing base. The original painted stencil was placed over the background colour print and registered with the new screen.

Each print in this edition is completely unique as there is so much variation in the coloured backgrounds.

The hand-painted acetate stencil that was used to create the photo stencil printing area.

The paper stencils were printed within the photo silkscreen open screen. About three layers of colour were added.

'The Grape Pickers'.

PROJECT: COMBINE A SIMPLE PHOTO STENCIL AND HAND-CUT PAPER STENCIL

I suggest that you experiment with different ways of stencil making by creating an A4, or similar, painted, printed or collaged piece of artwork. This will enable you to work out what works best in terms of print reproduction and how much detail you are able to capture on the screen.

Choose your own subject matter, but try lots of different mark-making materials to see how they work with the exposure unit and what you feel comfortable with.

EQUIPMENT AND MATERIALS

* Basic printing equipment
* Two screens (one coated with emulsion and one masked for paper pick-up stencils)
* Scissors
* Craft knife
* LED light box
* Paintbrushes
* Stencil film (cellophane, tracing paper, inkjet transparencies, drafting film etc.)
* Acrylic paint (black)
* Acrylic paint markers
* Indian ink
* Water-based wax crayons
* Printing paper (300gsm)
* Stencil paper or newspaper
* Printing ink

Method

Make a hand-painted positive that will be made into a photographic stencil and printed on top of a coloured paper stencil layer. You will need two screens. The paper stencil will be printed first and the photo stencil printed on top.

Paper stencils are used to create blocks of background colour. They have been torn to soften the edges of the print. The paper stencils were removed and repositioned, and colour has been painted on the screen using gouache and print binder.

Making the top stencil

Choose a stencil film and drawing material and place it over a design that will fit on the selected size of printing paper. This could contain an outline design or illustration, a selection of textures, or a mixture of both. Use different methods of mark-making and different materials. This will give a good indication of what works well when the positive is exposed.

Expose the screen

Expose the screen and let it dry prior to filling any pinholes and mask. Use the exposure guidelines and troubleshooting methods to reach the correct exposure time.

Make a paper-stencil print backdrop

Get creative with this step. You are essentially creating a background, so keep the colours in light and mid-tone values. Cut out or tear strips of paper and block out the screen. You can add more than one layer and introduce some monoprinting if you are feeling experimental.

Print the photo stencil

Make sure the paper-stencil layers are completely dry before printing the final photo stencil. Match up the photo stencil image with the background layers. This can be done by attaching the positive to one of the prints and registering it under the screen. Use the registration stops.

The final print uses the same top stencil, but all the background colours have unique colour variations.

PHOTO STENCILS: CAPTURING TONE

As already discussed, it can be very difficult to capture tone in the silkscreen printing process, although with patience and the right painting surface it is possible to recreate tonal variation.

Most films that are suitable for making analogue positives have a smooth surface and only capture opaque lines when exposed onto a screen. You can create the effect of tone by breaking up a painted line with scratching or splattering, but painted watercolour tones are impossible to achieve on surfaces such as Maylar and florists' acetate.

Specialised film products, however, have been designed to overcome this and replicate the textures and tonal variations that are associated with a stone lithograph. These films use a textured surface not unlike the surface of a lithographic stone. Pigment such as ink or graphite settles in the grain of the film, replicating a range of tones and hand-drawn marks. These films are made from polyester and can hold a mark from pencil, crayon, a paint wash and tonal rubbing, and produce a range of tones from dark to light.

Products that you can use include True-Grain and Mark Resist, both of which provide excellent results when used in conjunction with crayons, ink and paint. Textured tracing paper is also a good surface to work on, although, unlike film, painted and drawn marks are difficult to remove. True-Grain and Mark Resist can both be cleaned with methylated spirit and reused.

It is also possible to lightly sand drawing films and create your own surface.

My large silkscreen print 'On Guard' was an ambitious undertaking and used about fourteen different stencils to build up the design and colour. It was made using specialised acetates including True-Grain and Mark Resist, which were painted with Indian ink diluted with methylated spirits, then sanded and scratched to achieve lots of different textures.

The silkscreen print 'On Guard' was created using True-Grain stencils.

Design process

I have a small flock of guinea fowl on the farm where I live. They are totally wild and scurry around the garden and nearby pasture throughout the day, chatting and chasing one another, but always alert to danger. They are a constant source of amusement, and I often draw them when they visit my kitchen door for a quick drink or snoop through the window.

'On Guard' tries to capture their amusing and ever watchful temperament, particularly in the fields in late summer when the grass has been cut, and a hungry fox might be lurking in the hedgerow.

The origin of this print was a large collaged and painted artwork. I made all the elements of the design using hand-painted paper that I cut out and arranged on a large sheet of sugar paper. The birds take centre stage and descend in stature from left to right. They have some texture in their feathers, so it was important that marks featured throughout the piece. Two-thirds of the print is taken up with the birds, which are topped with a glowing hedgerow.

Stencil making

I had great fun making the stencils for this print. I started with the main design, copying it onto True-Grain by placing the original drawing underneath and painting the image with Indian ink.

I scraped away the ink to uncover the spotty feathers and scaly legs of the birds and to get some energy into the design. Each colour was painted onto the film and there is some collaged film on the trees, where I have painted film and cut it to shape. I have also knocked back some of the colours by printing white over some areas. There is a lot of layered printing and when you touch the print you can feel the textures.

Printing and registration

Although this was a big print, I cut up the stencils and printed it in sections. The light colours went down first, and I printed several reds and oranges on top of one another to create a thick deposit of ink on the birds' beaks and legs. As the under-colours spread across the print, I was able to melt the background ink under the birds' bodies.

This print was registered by fitting all the under-colours under the main stencil.

Original artwork design for 'On Guard'.

PROJECT: CAPTURING TONE

You will need to consider what surface to paint or draw on to capture tonal variations. If you refer to chapter 5 you will be able to consult the collage print that you made to determine what kind of marks you are able to pick up in your photo silkscreen prints. Painted marks are very different from marks made with a crayon. If you use True-Grain or Mark Resist it is easy to remove marks from the film surface using water or methylated spirits and start again, or simply wipe away sections to create highlights. Tracing paper. although a cheaper option, is more difficult to paint on top of, although it does take pencil and graphite exceptionally well.

True-Grain is excellent at picking up hand-drawn detail

EQUIPMENT AND MATERIALS

* Three screens, printing board
* Squeegee
* Palette knives
* Photo stencil equipment
* Three A4 sheets of acetate (True-Grain or Mark Resist) or tracing paper
* Indian ink, black wax crayon, black gouache etc.
* Paintbrushes
* Pot of water
* Methylated spirit
* Clean cloth
* Light box (optional)
* Inspiration, perhaps a hand-painted design or landscape
* Photo stencil materials
* Printing inks (three colours: dark, medium and light tones)

Method

Use a painterly design to replicate or use as inspiration. Create three painted or hand-drawn films representing the layers of the painting. You can mix and match the media, so don't just stick to paint or crayon. Imagine the layers you used to make the artwork in the first place and build the three stencils in the same way.

Dilute Indian ink to produce light, medium and dark washes and paint the individual layers using an expressive painting style that captures the quick marks made in watercolour painting.

The aim is to create a design in three layers that overlap one another. Your design can be completely abstract or based on an existing artwork.

Prepare the film

Cut three sheets of True-Grain or Mark Resist stencil material at A4 size or larger. Make sure the film extends over your design by 4cm. The two sides of the film have different textures: paint on the rough side. Number each piece of film.

Paint design

The ink can be diluted with water to achieve a wash that is applied directly to the film with a brush or sponge. Alternatively use a black water-based crayon and pick up the granular surface of the films. Water can also be added to the crayon. Each layer will be made into a photo stencil and printed with a specific colour. Therefore, each stencil needs to be made with the same intensity of pigment.

Add cross lines to the edge of each stencil and make sure these align. Cross lines can be covered up during printing and are used in the registration.

Make the photo stencils

You may need to experiment with exposure. Too short and the stencil will be weak and start to break down. Too long an exposure and the tonal detail will be lost, and you will get very little from the print.

Printing

Working from the under-colour to the top stencil, you can either use three different tones of the same colour or add other colours that pop out when the top stencil is printed. You can also include smearings of colour to add colour variations to different parts of the print.

Three stencils prior to printing.

Three prints showing tonal print development.

BONITO DEL NORTE
Raye
Poissonnier

CHAPTER 7

INTRODUCTION TO CREATING DIGITAL ARTWORK FOR SILKSCREEN PRINTING

Technology touches all our daily lives and the previous chapter explained how to make basic digital stencils for silkscreen printing using unsophisticated photography and photocopying. The process is straightforward and anyone with the right equipment should be able to copy an existing image and enlarge or reduce it in size, print it on acetate and make a photo stencil.

This chapter will go further and explain how digital skills can add value and creative depth to your creative projects. I will suggest a few free digital apps that can be used on a phone or tablet, are easy to use and may overcome some of the technological hurdles associated with more complex software.

The intention is to provide a basic overview, so don't expect a detailed guidebook on creative software. I have drawn on the help of other artists who utilise digital technology to create their artwork, generously sharing their thoughts about the use of digital technology in their creative work.

Previous chapters have concentrated on a wide range of analogue techniques that you can use to create silkscreen prints from your home studio and you should be familiar with them by now. All the areas that have been covered so far can be combined with digital artwork and should be considered when developing your designs.

Getting your designs out of a digital device and onto a transparency for silkscreen printing is not difficult, but you will need access to some equipment and specific materials if you are going to print at home. Be prepared to experiment and be realistic with the creative outcomes.

For the purposes of this chapter you will need a digital phone with a camera, a photo scanner and a tablet or computer. You will also need access to a printer that can make high-contrast stencils on acetate.

We will explore turning hand-drawn and painted artwork into digital files and undertake some minor manipulation. How you then use your digital transparencies when printed is subject to your own creativity, perhaps painting and scratching into the surface of the film or cutting out shapes to collage.

Keep in mind that using creative software requires an effort on your part to develop your own knowledge. I strongly recommend experimenting with new technology to develop your skills. Hopefully there will be something for everyone in this chapter, whether you are an experienced digital native, keen to upgrade your skills, or just finding your way and want some basic knowledge to get started.

Digital collage 'Poissonnier'.

Landscape print by artist James Bywood.

OVERVIEW

There are so many different creative software packages available for tablets, computers and phones. Those that can perform more professional tasks generally require a subscription and unless you are working within the design industry you will probably find little use for them. However, a designer branching out into silkscreen printing may find that several basic print and design considerations covered in this chapter might prove useful.

I don't use any specific creative software on my computer, and I get by with basic photo and app functions on both my desktop and tablet. These enable me to resize scanned images of artwork, layout posters or greetings cards, set text and perform some basic image manipulation such as creating halftones. I haven't yet managed to make the move from hand to digital drawing as I find it difficult to make expressive marks of a similar quality with a digital pencil and associated tools.

My process generally starts by compiling black-and-white imagery onto a white paper background. I use a range of techniques including black fine-liner ink as well as black-and-white photocopies to generate my designs. I also use my own black-and-white photographs of objects and sketchbook drawings, which I print onto paper and cut and paste into place.

Layout page apps are very useful if you are considering small, illustrated publications, as you can easily arrange and resize your work to a specific print size and bring in digital images without resorting to scissors and glue.

My printer is a basic A4 office inkjet, so if I need to output my artwork on anything larger, I prepare it for digital printing and send it to my local print shop.

It should be noted that most high-street print shops don't print onto acetate, so I take my stock with me.

DIGITAL FILE TYPES

The several digital file types that will be referred to in this chapter have different properties. As this is a basic introduction, the examples and projects that I have set will use bitmap files that can be made with limited software and manipulated on a computer, tablet or phone. The approach concentrates on using hand-drawn artwork as a starting point, combined with photographs and collage.

Raster or bitmap files

The process of turning a handmade drawing or design into a digital image requires a computer scanner or camera. The design is transferred into a digital file, such as a JPEG, which consists of a matrix of small dots or pixels that make

'Garden Views' is a three-colour print and combines a digital photo stencil taken from a sketchbook printed light green and overprinted with two hand-painted stencils in dark green and magenta.

up the image. If you zoom into a bitmap image the edges will look lumpy. When bitmap images are enlarged, they can appear blurry.

Bitmap images are either pure black or white and are digitally printed on to acetate and used in the same way as handmade stencils. Digital stencils can be combined with analogue/handmade transparencies during the photo stencil making process. Areas of a digital stencil, for example, can be cut and collaged onto a handmade stencil or combined during the printing process.

Vector files

Vector is a term describing artwork that has been created in programmes such as Adobe Illustrator and is based on plotting the outlines of shapes using lines and points rather than pixels. Vector graphics create a clean and infinitely scalable design.

Artist and printmaker Nikki Williams (aka The 'Print Lass') creates her artwork using vectors and describes her process later in this chapter.

Nikki's strong digital designs are hand-drawn in Adobe Illustrator, creating vector shapes and lines that she fills with colour.

TURNING ANALOGUE INTO DIGITAL

Analogue/handmade black-and-white designs can easily be turned into digital bitmapped files. You can also use a coloured drawing from a sketchbook or a design with a high contrast and turn it into a black-and-white image using basic photo software on a computer or phone.

Consider how large you want to make your finished prints. If your artwork is A4 and you want to enlarge it to a finished A2 print size, you may experience bitmapping, which is evident in the loss of sharpness on the edges of the image.

I use my A4 scanner/printer for small black-and-white designs that I send to my computer for basic manipulation.

Sketchbook drawings of an old camera with a limited colour palette were easy to digitise and turn into stencils for screen print.

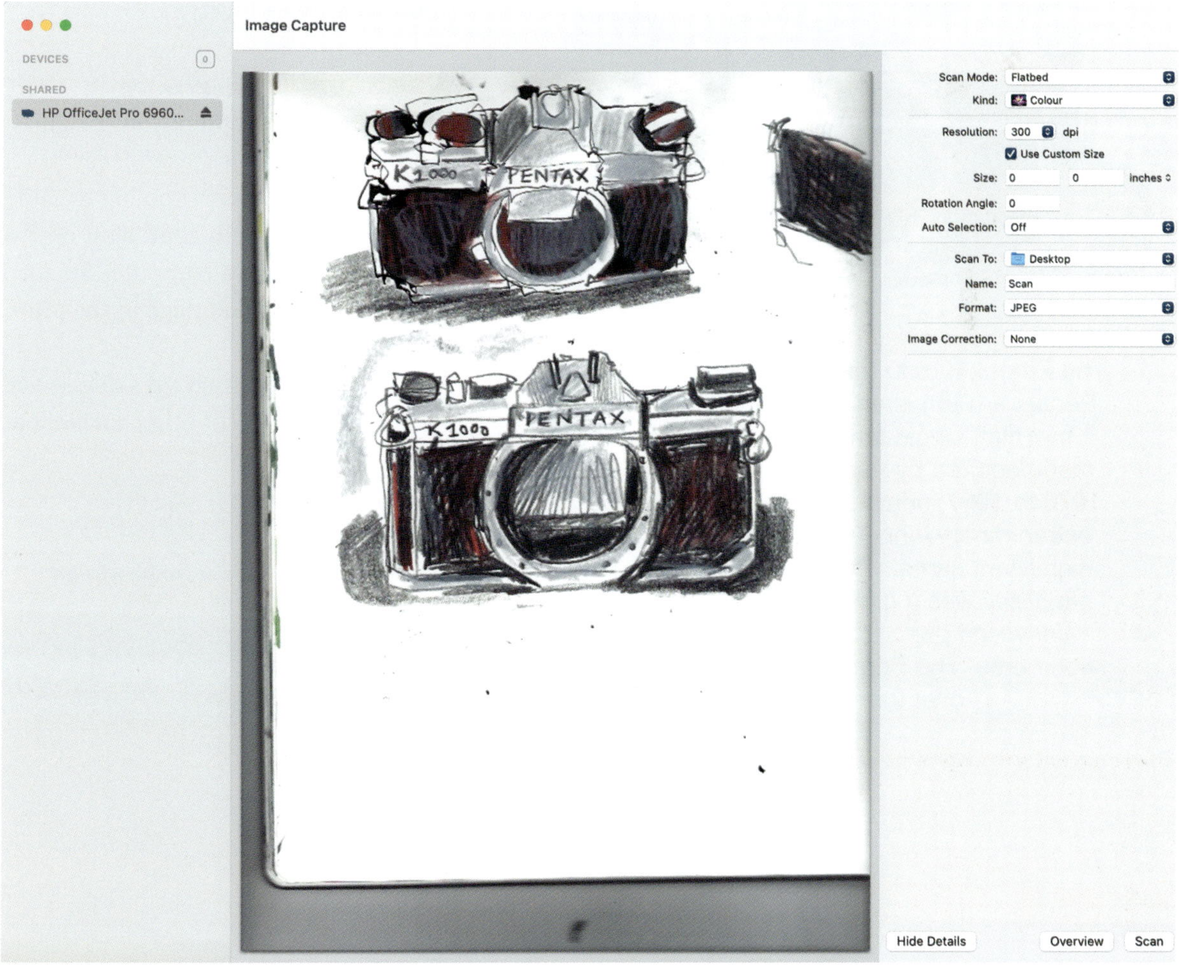

Scanned sketchbook drawing imported into basic computer software and cropped to size.

After cropping the image is desaturated and turned into a black-and-white image, saved as a JPEG and printed.

The Pentax K1000 (originally marked the Asahi Pentax K1000) is an interchangeable lens, 35 mm film, single-lens reflex (SLR) camera, manufactured by Asahi Optical Co., Ltd. from 1976 to 1997, originally in Japan. The K1000's extraordinary longevity makes it a historically significant camera. The K1000's inexpensive simplicity was a great virtue and earned it an unrivalled popularity as a basic but sturdy workhorse. The Pentax K1000 eventually sold over three million units.

Combining text with a digital image using a basic computer program.

The scanned image is imported into a basic photo manipulation program and the contrast of the image is increased. If the image is in colour, it can be converted to greyscale and the contrast increased. Other changes can also be made, such as converting the image into a negative or cropping it.

Setting up a basic print layout

When working on a basic computer layout programme, start by setting up a page and importing the JPEG image. Adjust the size and position of the image and add text and any other features. The file can then be converted into a JPEG or PDF and output by an inkjet printer.

Artwork needs to be sized correctly for the silkscreen frame you are using. The following table lists screen sizes that will fit specific page and artwork sizes. Note that 'Page Size' can be edited in 'Page Settings' or 'Document Settings'.

Photographing analogue designs

Taking a photograph of your original artwork using a phone or digital camera is a useful way to reduce large black-and-white designs that are too big to fit in an A4 scanner. Simply photograph them in good light on a white background and send them to a computer for manipulation. You can also manipulate an image in the phone before sending it to your computer.

This process is very versatile as very large images can be reduced to fit other surfaces and sizes and avoid bitmapped edges.

Screen size	Page size (width × height)	Max. artwork size (width × height)
32 × 32cm	21 × 29.7cm	19 × 19cm
A3	29.7 × 42cm	27.7 × 40cm
A3+	33 × 48.3cm	31 × 46.3cm
A2	42 × 59.4cm	40 × 57.4cm

Creating tonal images

It is difficult to print tonal images when working in silkscreen. Halftones create the impression of tone and texture by digitally turning a design into lots of tiny dots. Some are closer together, giving the impression of a dark tone, whereas others are spread out reflecting a medium or light tone.

Halftones can also be used creatively, and you can distort images by increasing the dot size and reducing the design to a graphic image.

If you don't have access to software that can reproduce artwork using halftones, a print shop may be able to undertake the work for you. Artwork should be the actual size you want to print in PDF or JPEG format with a resolution of 300dpi.

This lobster design was created from a large black-and-white painting, then photographed, saved at 300dpi and digitally reduced to fit T-shirts, tote bags and cards.

The purple top layer of this print is a halftone. The darker areas of the print are made up of dots that are close together and the tonal areas with dots that are further apart.

Black-and-white design of camera with a large halftone.

CREATING HALFTONES WITH PROCREATE

You can easily convert your images into halftones using a number of digital programs and apps that are easily available at reasonable expense. If you have an image with a wide range of tonal values that you want to capture in your print you can use the halftone process to do this.

The app used in this example is Procreate, which is available for iPads only, and Procreate Pocket for iPhones. Similar apps should be available for Android, Chrome, Windows and Linux tablets.

Method

Make sure you have chosen an image with good tonal values. Import it into Procreate from a mobile phone or other device. Procreate supplies a range of image manipulation options and you can choose how big and what size halftone you want.

After manipulation the image is saved as a JPEG or PDF. The chosen format can then be shared to a computer or distributed by email.

Analogue halftones

There are other ways of using halftones within your work without making a digital file. You can simply download a halftone design from the internet, print it on acetate or paper and apply it to an analogue stencil as a fill or shape. Newsprint text or images also work well as halftones are applied as part of the printing process. Simpley photocopy it onto film and cut and paste into your stencil.

EQUIPMENT AND MATERIALS

You can either output your stencil using a home printer or send your artwork to a print bureau for output on a laser copier. If you are using the latter method, make sure it is compatible with the printer.

* iPad with Procreate installed
* Artwork, preferably with high contrast as very fine washes are difficult to replicate
* Scanner or phone camera
* Printer (optional)
* Transparency film for printing (optional)

A photo cut from a magazine was used in the creation of this bird print. The halftone is difficult to detect as it is so small. Notice how well it has captured tone.

Original colour artwork was chosen to turn into a halftone. It was scanned at 300dpi.

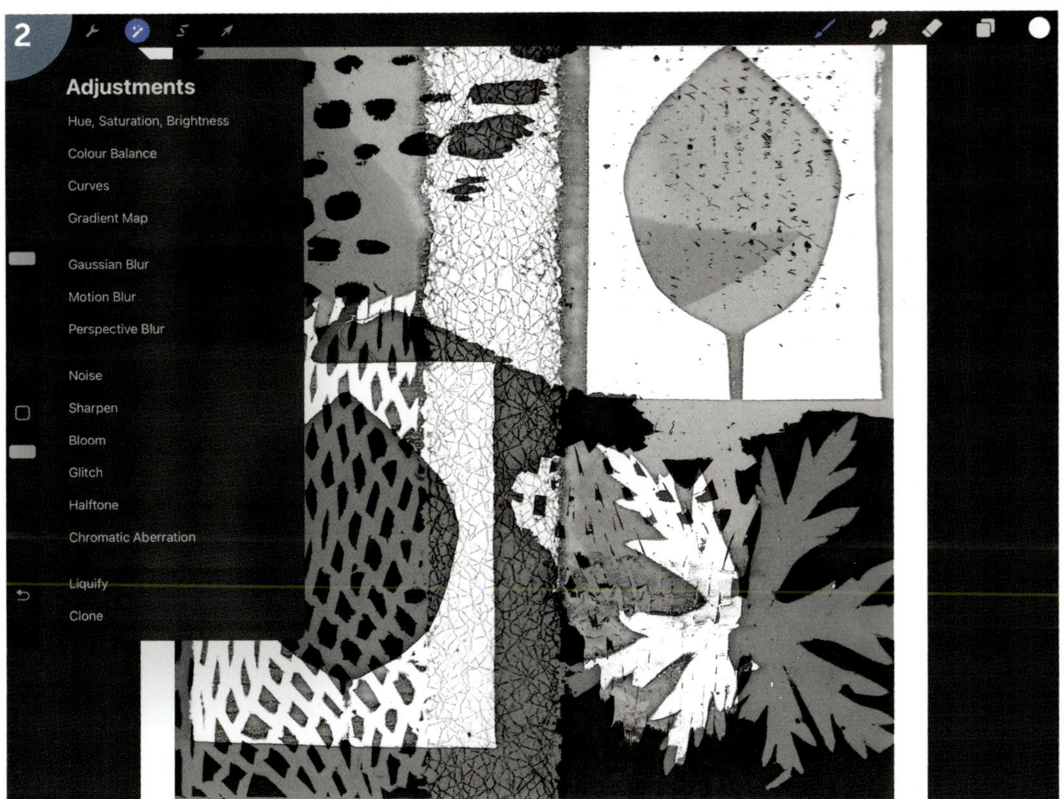

The colour image was turned into a black-and-white image, and the contrast was increased.

Using Procreate, set up a page in the size you want to print and insert the photograph. Go to the adjustments menu and click on halftone, move the slider top-left to increase the halftone size by the percentage required and set the bottom bar for silkscreen print. The photo shows the halftone level set at 4% and 8%.

DESIGN USING LAYOUT SOFTWARE

One you have mastered digitising your artwork and you have a collection of JPEGs on a computer, it is easy to use an online app such as Canva to paste them into a digital design space on a computer. The app will allow you to set up a custom size page, split it into columns, add text and bring in images. It allows you to visualise the printed design in colour and make separations on further pages. Images need to be black and white, and blocks of colour can be added, then turned to monochrome before outputting as a stencil.

Canva is an online graphic design tool available in iOS format for iPads and iPhones, and also for Android, Windows, Chromebook and Mac devices, so it can be used on desktop computers, laptops, mobile phones and tablets. The basic app is free, but there are also paid annual subscription options if that does not meet all your needs. It uses a drag and drop interface, is simple to use and is great for posters or greetings cards. You can set up a custom size, add a photo, crop, save your image as a JPEG or PDF and send it to print. It also includes some useful filters. A description of how to set up a page using Canva to design small publications, cards and zines will be found in Chapter 8.

Collate a collection of black-and-white JPEG images in a folder on your computer. Text can be pasted into the design and it's a good idea to create this before you start your design.

Design ideas can be worked up to the size of the print or in the same ratio on paper, but the convenience of being able to move elements around the digital design interface makes this a winning option.

Method

Despite its flexibility, I have found that the most efficient way to work with Canva is on a computer. Decide on the purpose of your design, such as a greetings card or poster. Work out the size of the finished print, the number of colours and any other factors, such as how many folds there will be in the paper and where the front and back will be. Sometimes a paper mock-up is a good way of deciding which way up images should go too.

This method will explain how to design an A3 two-colour (blue and black) poster in Canva incorporating a black-and-white image and some text.

Open Canva and set up a custom page size

I have set my page to A3 portrait (page number 1) and added a border and two columns. This is a fundamental design basic and will give you the structure to add all your design elements.

Place the digital images

Keep black-and-white JPEG images in a folder on your desktop and simply drag them into position on the Canva design page and resize.

Add a second colour

You can add simple shape blocks and colour across the design on the same page and visualise what the design will look like. Keep the colours to a simple fit with the other printed elements.

Add text

Text can be pasted from a Word document into the design where it is easy to manipulate.

Split the print colours
Copy and paste your design onto a new page. You can now start to remove all the top colours, so you are left with the colour layer. Turn all the design elements black.

Save design
Turn design into a printable PDF and output onto acetate.

Other free photo and design apps

There is a multitude of apps that can be used to digitise your design, create artwork or apply different effects. Most are free, although many functions may require a subscription. Beware of tools that take away your creative instinct or draw you into the world of AI.

Adobe Photoshop Express Photo Editor is available as an app for iOS (iPads and iPhones), Android, Chromebook and Windows, but you should be aware that the free Windows version has less functionality than the other platforms, and even they vary as to how much can be done before you come up against a subscription barrier. The free versions, nonetheless, can edit photos and drawings and are easy to use. Among the tasks they can perform is inserting text into your work and cropping, distorting and reshaping images.

Another long-term Adobe program, Lightroom Photo Editor, supports more features but is now only available on monthly or annual subscription. Anyone seeking the ability to work with RAW files from their camera, but without a subscription, should look at RawTherapee (macOS, Windows and Linux).

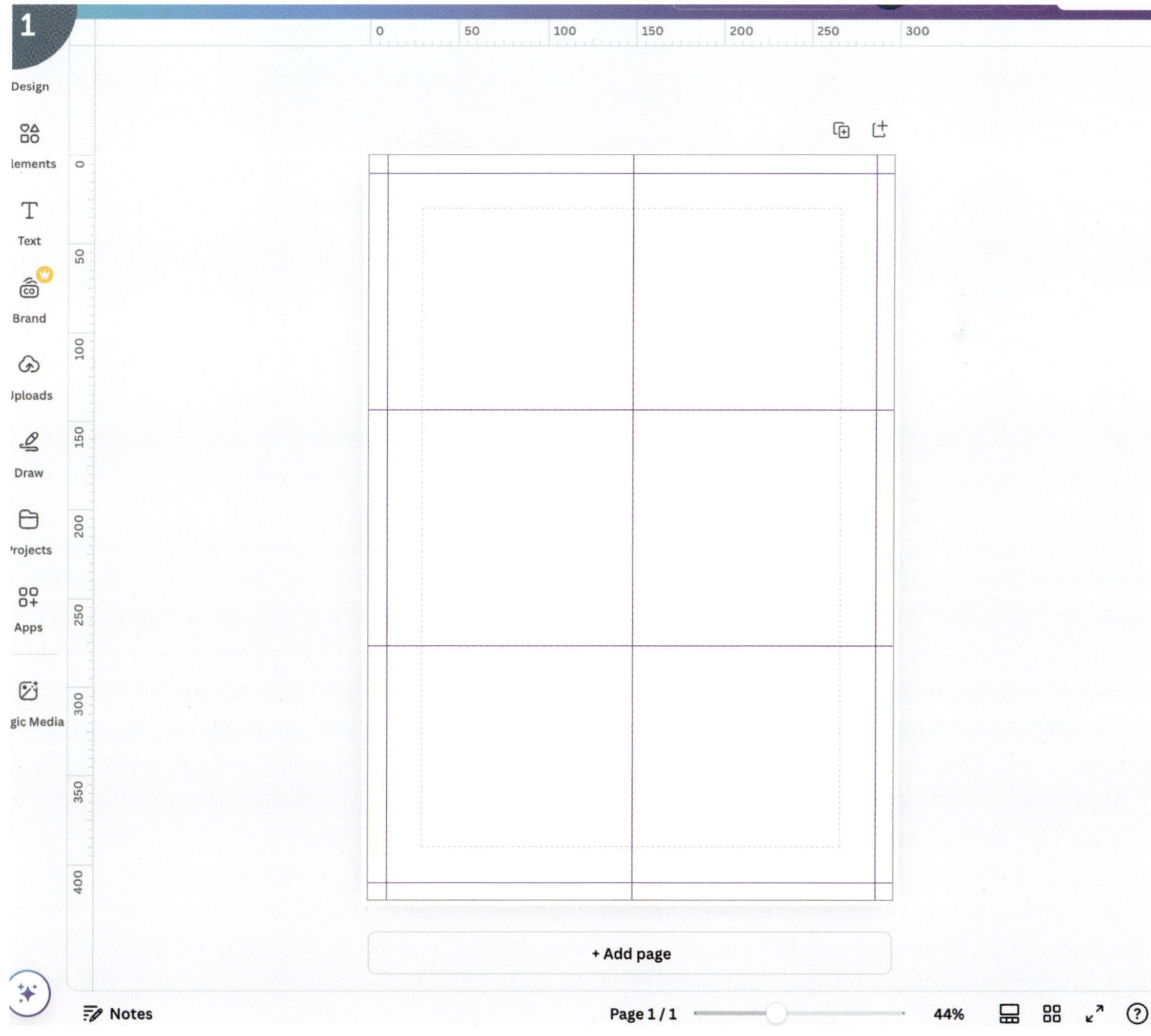

Set up an A3 page in Canva.

2

Insert image and text. When using the design features in the app, experiment with elements such as coloured blocks and reversing the text.

PRINTING TRANSPARENCIES FOR SILKSCREEN

It is easy to output a digital image to transparent film using a compatible home inkjet printer, although I choose to send mine to a local copy shop as their photocopier gives much better results than my inkjet printer. Set your artwork at 300 or 600dpi for finer detail and send it as a PDF.

If printing from home, ensure that you buy the correct film for your printer and set the printer for high contrast on glossy paper. You may need to experiment with this as some printer inks are darker than others. You may want to invest in a home printer that can output larger than A4. There are also online options that can copy your work professionally and post them back to you. Make sure you read all their digital requirements before using this option.

Right size of digital artwork and mesh size

Resolution, or the amount of detail you can capture in photo silkscreen prints, can be described as high or low. How much detail can be captured in a screen print is dependent on the mesh size. In order to print high-resolution digital designs you will need a mesh size that has a high mesh count.

High resolution or more detail will require a mesh size of 120 or above, whereas most prints can be accommodated on a 90 mesh.

Mesh relates to how many threads per centimetre: 120T, for example, has 120 threads per centimetre. Typography at smaller point sizes, for example 12 to 14 point, will require a 120 mesh for best results as will fine lines.

3

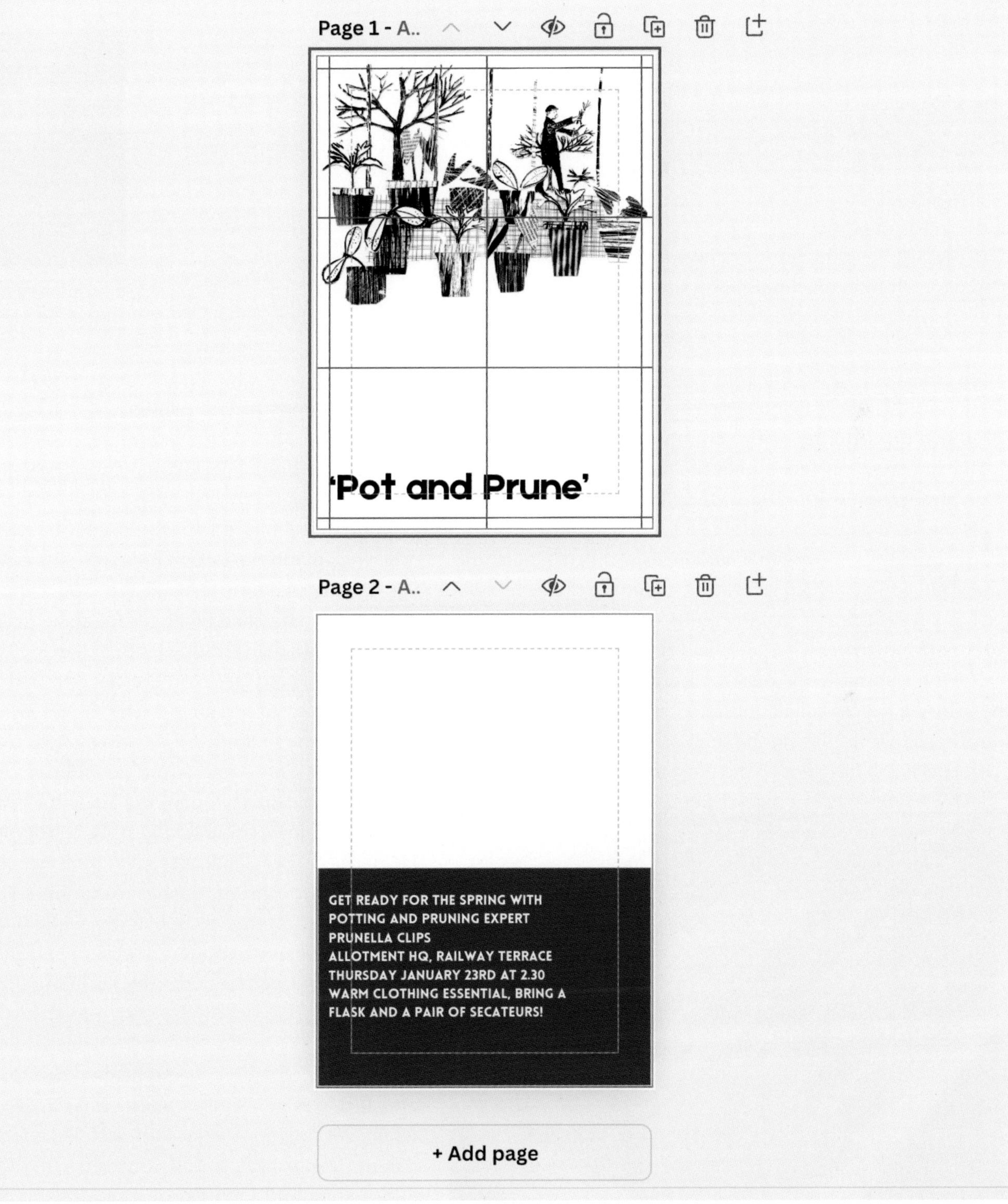

Create a second page and turn all the print elements black.

Artist and printmaker James Bywood.

PROFILE: JAMES BYWOOD

jamesbywood.co.uk

Artist James Bywood describes how he creates hand-drawn images on his iPad using Procreate and prepares them for print.

James is a Leeds-based illustrator and printmaker. He has a home studio where he makes striking limited-edition silkscreen prints of the British countryside, combining both digital and analogue techniques to craft images that are full of dramatic compositions and vibrant colour choices.

James has a degree in fine art, but his route into printmaking came through a beginner's print-making adult education course, which reintroduced him to the process. He has always enjoyed making multiples and selling his work at print fairs.

Having a home studio enables him to experiment with the printing process, make mistakes and generally have fun. He enjoys not having the time constraints of renting a print space and has created a compact professional working studio equipped with a small vacuum printing bench, exposure lamps and A2 printer.

'Tall Trees', a silkscreen print by James Bywood.

James has always enjoyed the silkscreen medium because of its quick, positive process, which suits his expressive, painterly way of working. Originally working in sketchbooks, he was an early adopter of creative software and, working in the design industry, was accustomed to working digitally. He learned a lot about the transition from digital file to finished print, although he makes the point that there are many pathways to achieving the same result using digital software. You just need to find the one that suits your way of working.

James uses an iPad and drawing pencil to digitally create his artwork. Photographs and sketchbooks are his starting point, and he aims to adapt the analogue process using digital technology mimicking stone lithography and linocut. He has become very accustomed to drawing on an iPad, adapting the drawing brushes to suit his style.

He makes layered compositions while referring to the photo reference that he keeps on his iPad. Starting with the top layer, he begins by outlining the image, carefully working in on the design to create textures and interesting surfaces.

A palette of colours is established, which he refers to and also uses in his other work. This ensures consistency when working on a series of prints. He refers to the colour palette and carefully mixes his inks to match. Subsequent under-colours are created on new layers. Prior to printing his transparencies each layer is turned into a black-and-white image.

James outputs his transparencies on an A2 inkjet printer/plotter and continues to work into them by applying handmade marks. Each colour layer is carefully matched with the palette and printed in sequence. This is where he has total control over the ink tone and hue and can tweak the finished design.

Tablet, drawing pencil and brushes.

Adding texture in Procreate.

Turning the blue layer of the design into black to output as a transparency.

Artist and printmaker Nikki Williams (aka the 'Print Lass').

PROFILE: NIKKI WILLIAMS

theprintlass.co.uk

Artist Nikki Williams (aka 'The Print Lass') takes us into her studio and explains her design process using Adobe Illustrator.

Nikki is a designer and printmaker working from her home studio in Keighley, where she has a simple silkscreen print set-up and design space. Nikki is inspired by mid-twentieth-century architecture and decorative arts and makes colourful concertina cards, three-dimensional printed wooden panels and limited-edition prints.

She has a homemade exposure unit and cleans her screens outside on her patio in the dog's bath. She uses a homemade print board and five screens that are all the same size and fit neatly under her desk. A simple but striking colour scheme runs throughout her work with a colour palette that changes depending on the season.

Her journey into the creative sector started at school where she fell in love with print and went on to do a degree in the decorative arts. She runs her small business from home and uses digital programmes such as Illustrator and Photoshop to create her designs. She gained her digital knowledge through online courses, initially learning how

Nikki's concertina house design.

Nikki's studio with exposure unit.

to transfer designs onto textiles for manufacture. She says that working digitally switched her brain on to working in layers and this has made it easy for her to transition to silkscreen printing.

Although she uses a computer and iPad to make final artwork, her designs start out as simple sketches, which she translates into colourful paper models before crossing over into digital. She also makes analogue textures that she scans into her computer to use in her final design. She enjoys creating silkscreen overlays and textures in this way. Nikki describes her process as outlining shapes, applying a fill, then using digital scissors to cut out shapes for collage.

Nikki refers to her paper models during the design process, placing them in front of the computer screen as reference and inspiration. She tends to work in two colours (black and red) initially. Her iPad is also linked to her computer, which she uses for sketching and expressive mark-making. She says that she 'enjoys the freedom that it gives her to make a mistake and go back a step'. Nikki is finding that technology is changing all the time, which can be a challenge if you are not using it on a regular basis. She also highlights that it can restrict free play, which is why she works on her own cut-out models and collage.

Nikki's tablet is connected to her computer to enable her to draw fine detail.

Nikki uses analogue cut-outs as inspiration in the design process.

PROJECT: DIGITAL PHOTO COMPOSITE PRINT

This is an easy way to get started combining digital and analogue methods in one artwork for photo silkscreen printing. Let your creativity go wild and look at how you can combine a wide range of images, text and handmade drawings and designs. Cut and reassemble your elements and give them a new meaning, setting them in a fantasy landscape or a hand-painted backdrop.

You will need access to a printer and plenty of source material, such as sketchbooks, old prints, newspapers, maps and magazines. Try to work from your own original material if possible. You can also combine your own black-and-white photographs.

All printing and stencil-making equipment and materials will also be required to print the finished artwork.

Method

This method is basically a 'cut and paste' process using materials that you have copied digitally using a phone or similar device, printed onto white paper, then cut and reassembled in a physical design area. 'Paste-ups' like this were the forerunners of the current digital design industry and are an easy alternative to using design software while embracing some accessible digital tools.

You will be working within an A3 or A4 format, so make sure that your design will fit within these constraints, and you also have screens that can accommodate the sizes.

The aim is to create a bold design that can be printed on top of one or two under-colours. The under-colours can be created using painted acetates or from other digital stencils using the same photomontage methods described. You may want to choose a theme and collect material that reflects this. Decide on whether it will be portrait or landscape orientation.

A collection of collage materials on a 'fishy' theme.

EQUIPMENT AND MATERIALS

Printing Materials and Equipment

* 2 screens and baseboard and all Photo silkscreen equipment
* Printing inks (2 tones)
* Printing paper

Design and Stencil making

* Smartphone with a camera and photo app and/or a digital SLR camera with SD card
* Stencil output options, such as access to a copy shop, photocopier or inkjet printer. Online print options should also be considered
* Transparent film compatible with your printer
* Sketchbooks, old books/typography, newsprint, old music, maps etc.
* White card or board for pasting your design (optional)
* Acrylic pens (black)
* Black ink or paint and brushes
* Glue stick
* Transparent film for painting, such as Maylar

In my print 'Poissonnier' I have combined physical objects including a ceramic fish platter and some food packaging with a car boot sale print and one of my own silkscreen prints. I also photographed some net to include in a printed backdrop.

I made two stencils: a simple pale-blue background was overprinted with dark blue. The print size was A3, and the top stencil printed at a copy shop. The under-colour was split into two A4 acetates, which were then stuck together.

Assembling and copying collage materials

All the collected material should be photographed in good light or scanned to a computer or tablet. Images can be enlarged or reduced to fit your design.

Place the artwork on a scanner or photocopier, scan at 300dpi and save as a JPEG. Send to your computer, tablet or phone and change the image to black and white. Try increasing the contrast of the image to produce a good opaque stencil. If you have access to Procreate or similar photo manipulation apps, try the halftone option or other effects.

Alternatively, take a photograph using a digital camera. Phone cameras will provide good enough results for this method. Make sure that you place the artwork on a light background in good, even daylight, if possible. Manipulate the image as before after turning into a black-and-white image.

Try copying three-dimensional objects using a digital camera or use an existing photograph of a landscape or a sketchbook drawing. Turn the image to black and white and manipulate on a computer, camera or tablet as described. You can capture shadows during this process, and they work well. I turned my fish image and net into a halftone and used it as my backdrop.

Cut and paste

After copying and digitizing your materials, send them to a printer and output on white paper. Remember that your images need to be black and white if you are going to turn them into a stencil for silkscreen. Halftone images should be printed in the same way. Experiment with dot size and how you can capture tone.

Decide on how many colours you want to print and lay out your design to the print size on white card. Cut up your images with a pair of scissors or a scalpel and find new ways to put them back together. Consider focal points and try to convey a message or story. Try adding some text or make some hand-painted textures. These can be included as well.

When you are happy with the design positions, glue the black and white collage pieces to the white background. Thick white card will ensure that your collaged papers remain flat.

Repeat for the under-colour. I copied my under-colour designs directly onto two sheets of A4 acetate. Think about overlaying colours and how this will change the impact of your design.

Stencil making and printing

Output your finished designs onto acetates ready for exposure on separate screens and print.

Assemble collage material.

Photograph the collaged items in good light using a mobile phone.

Three-dimensional objects can also be photographed and incorporated.

Images can be turned into halftones.

Copy collaged artwork onto thin paper.

Copy collage artwork onto film.

Print the turquoise blue under-colour.

Printing the dark blue top colour.

Angela's Little Book of Ornament

CHAPTER 8

SCREEN PRINTING: OTHER CREATIVE USES, FINISHING AND EDITIONING

Screen printing has diversified over the years. While traditionally it was used to print on textiles and paper, the process has been and remains a multi-surface printing technique. While it has been superseded by digital printing, it is still used by many artists and designers to embellish items such as jewellery, wood, handmade textiles, furnishings and stationery.

This chapter will offer an insight into some of the methods used to print onto multiple surfaces and how this can be achieved in your home set-up. We also delve into the world of self-published zines and small booklets and harness a range of digital layout software that can make the design and printing job easier.

There are several tasks where you can test your skills. Artist Suzi Thompson explains the methods, equipment and materials for making a simple stitched book cover and notebook. Other projects include constructing three-dimensional shapes from printed papers, greetings cards and basic textile printing.

Artists Zoë Eady and Lilly Kellett both give detailed insights into the techniques they use for silkscreen printing onto wood and creating under-colours for lino prints respectively, and explain their printing methods.

You will discover that most of the printing techniques already discussed can be modified along with the equipment and materials. While other publications may give a more detailed approach to printing onto specific materials, it is to be hoped that this chapter will pique your interest and make you want to learn more.

Finishing techniques such as trimming and tearing paper, paper storage, paper folding and stitching are also covered, some within the specific processes at the beginning of the chapter and others within the finishing section.

The final section of this book takes an informative look at the formal process of editioning your work. Understanding how to sign and number your work is an important part of the printing process that shows the unique number of prints available within the edition size and gives other important information about the print.

Silkscreen-printed wooden decorations.

Silkscreen-printed zine.

SMALL BOOKS, ZINES, CARDS AND THREE-DIMENSIONAL MOBILES

Silkscreen printing is a great way of sharing your creativity with a wider audience through handmade magazines, pamphlets, cards and books. Having something that you can hold in your hand or display is also much more tangible and tactile for readers. Self-publishing small print runs that share your ideas and skills can help you connect with others who share your viewpoint and offer them a greater understanding of your creative process.

In this chapter we will look at how versatile the silkscreen process is in the production of folded and three-dimensional decorative artwork as illustrated in the following ways:

* How to create an 8-page illustrated zine
* Greetings cards
* How to stitch a small booklet with a printed cover
* Project: Folding a three-dimensional Christmas Star

We will look at the skills and equipment required to fold and sculpt paper and card and how you can use free digital tools to improve the layout of your designs in preparation for printing.

Each of these projects requires specific equipment and materials that are listed in each section. You can use a range of different printing techniques too. I have included photo silkscreen, monoprinting and filler techniques, but this can be adapted to suit your printing set-up.

I made the zine using Canva, an app already introduced in Chapter 7, and I have included the template shapes and folding techniques. I suggest you familiarize yourself with the specific folds before you start as they will be referred to in the description.

Folding techniques

It is essential to master various folding techniques used in origami that will be employed in this section. You may also need to fold your prints, for example if you have made your own cards or created a folded zine or other printed publication.

Make sure your hands are clean and that you are working on a smooth, hard surface. The paper crease should be clean and sharp, and you should use a bone folder to apply even pressure. Make sure the edges match up by doing a soft fold (a gentle fold without creasing).

The main fold types are known as 'mountain' and 'valley', commonly referred to as a book fold.

Made of one piece of paper, an eight-page folded zine is an easy way of creating a small booklet.

Basic book fold: fold the paper in half, edge to edge, to form a middle crease.

'Mountain' fold: fold the top edge down to achieve a mountain shape.

'Valley' fold: fold the edges together to achieve a valley shape.

'Shawl' fold: fold the paper on the diagonal and crease.

'Gate' fold: fold the paper in half, then fold each side flap into the middle. The finished fold looks like a gate.

'Kite' fold: make three folds to create a kite shape. Fold diagonal edges to a central fold.

DESIGNING AND PRINTING AN EIGHT-PAGE FOLDING ZINE

Zines, short for magazines, are easy to create. Silkscreen offers a handmade process that maintains the limited-edition and unique nature of the publication. Zines can be one page of paper folded or a multi-folded concertina. The contents can be anything you wish, including hand illustrations, poetry, photographs and collage. Subject matter could be a seasonal guide to your own personal recipes with space to add notes, a story, an illustrated song or a collection of art prints.

Small uncomplicated designs that are laid out on simple folded sheets are a good place to start with no more than two colours. If you utilise the white of the paper, then one colour might be enough.

Consider different methods of folding an A3 or A4 sheet of paper and how a design may travel across it. You can print on one side or create a double-sided print.

You can also consider the message you want to convey and how will it translate into a silkscreen print. You can hand-paint or draw a stencil or use a digital layout program to insert images reduced in size to fit.

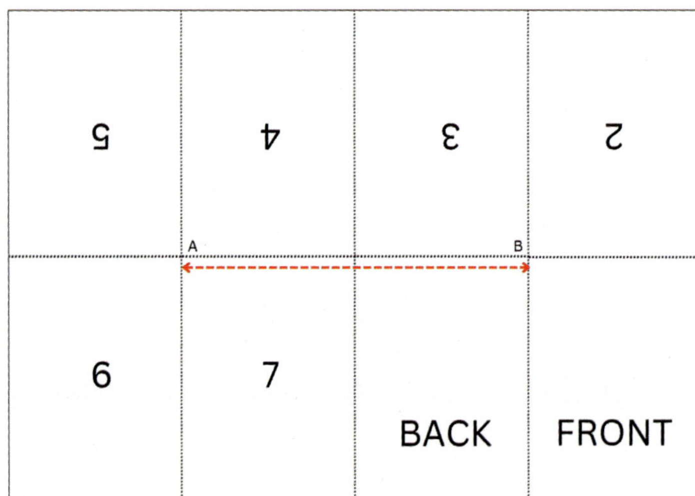

Use this template to help you lay out your zine. Notice where the front and back covers are located.

Method

This simple one-page layout folds into a small booklet. In this case I have silkscreen printed it on A3 125gsm paper as it is easy to fold when printed and a good size to view. The folding method enables 8 pages of illustrations, which I have copied and carried over into the design app Canva. The design has been split into two colours and incorporates blocks of background colour and text.

This layout can be used as a double-sided concertina pullout or card, or as a double-sided four-page booklet.

You can also use this template to make an analogue stencil. Simply use the template and overlay your painted artwork on acetate to create the positive.

Ensure your designs are in the right orientation (the right way up when the zine is folded) and make sure multiple colours line up.

Template

The template for the eight-page folding zine consists of four double pages, including the cover and back page. The design is laid out in landscape orientation. The designs on the top of the page are flipped upside down and will turn the right way up when the paper is 'mountain' folded.

EQUIPMENT AND MATERIALS

* All printing equipment including photo silkscreen
* Trimming equipment (cutting board and sharp craft knife, metal ruler)
* Bone folder
* Desktop computer (using the Canva website)
* Good-quality printing paper (120gsm)
* Printing inks (two colours)

Digital layout

I created an A3 page in Canva, splitting it into four equal columns and including a small border. The design was created in black and red, but I also included the white of the paper by reversing some of the text. I used this as my master copy and created two further A3 pages, copying the design onto both.

Splitting the design into two stencils

I removed all the red from the first page, leaving the black design. I then selected and removed all the black design areas on the second page and turned them black too. I was left with the two separate breakdown stencils for photo silkscreen that I turned into high-quality PDFs. I also added trim marks as the colour registration was very tight, which reduced the size of the print by around 4cm.

Making and printing the stencils

The stencils were placed side by side on a large screen in a portrait orientation. I then printed on paper that was larger than the design as trim marks had been included and I wanted to be able to handle the edge of the paper. The red colour was printed first, taking care to flood and pull only once. Overwetting the thin paper will cause it to cockle out of shape and it will not dry flat. I used the acetate method of registration for the second colour, lining up the colours using the trim marks as well as tweaking some areas to fit around the red shapes.

Cutting and folding the zine

Cut the zine out of the paper using a scalpel and metal ruler. You can also use a rotary trimmer to speed up the process.

Canva is a useful app for laying out basic designs. You can scale, flip and colour your artwork.

The digital artwork was output on two separate A3 transparencies.

When cutting the zine from paper, use trim marks to ensure that the cut is accurate.

Fold the zine in half using a 'Book' fold and unfold.

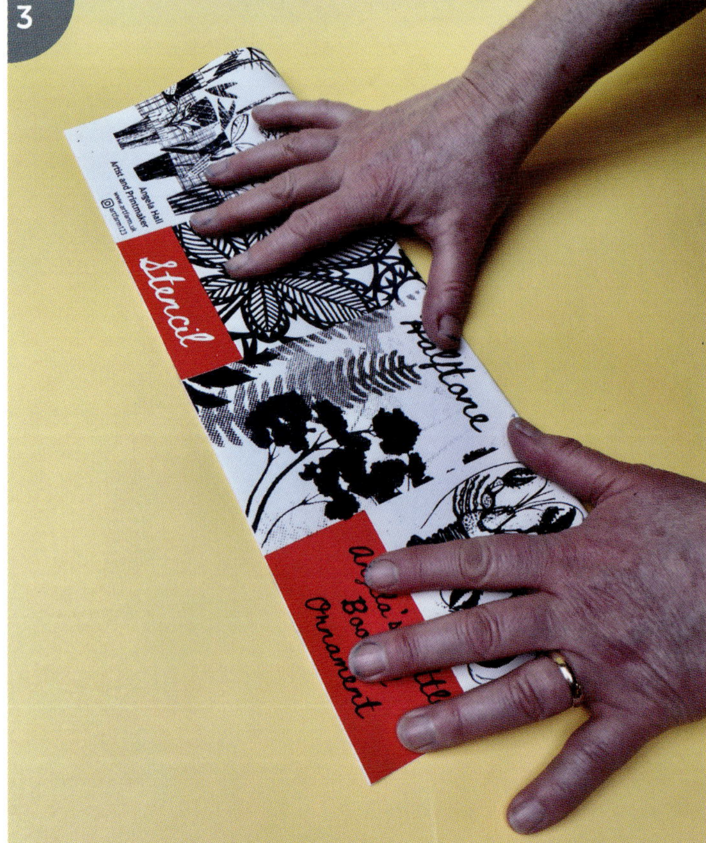

Fold the zine in half horizontally using a 'Mountain' fold and unfold.

Fold the zine in the middle using the 'Gate' fold and unfold.

Fold the zine in half again using the 'Book' fold. Cut through the middle of the first column from the folded edge and unfold.

Fold the zine into the 'Mountain' fold again and squeeze both ends. The middle section will start to gape like the mouth of a baby bird.

Further squeezing will create a windmill of four back-to-back pages with the front and back pages wrapping around the two in the middle.

Fold the four pages into position. When all the pages are aligned, press the zine under a heavy weight overnight.

PROFILE: SUZI THOMPSON

Artist Suzi Thompson working in her garden studio.

suzithompson.co.uk

Suzi Thompson is fine art printmaker based in South Yorkshire working with collagraph, drypoint and relief printing processes to create limited edition prints, artists' books and a range of hand printed, bound and stitched notebooks.

Printmaker Suzi Thompson trained as a goldsmith and turned to printmaking more than fifteen years ago after attending a ten-week course at the West Yorkshire Print Workshop. Working in collagraph, which she found a very accessible option to continue at home, she eventually started to become overwhelmed with prints that were 'not up to scratch'. Taking a sidestep, she found that she could put her three-dimensional skills to good use and started to make small handmade books incorporating her beautiful collagraph prints as the wraparound covers.

Although she is not professionally trained in bookbinding, she has managed to use her practical skills to create highly individual notebooks that she sells through galleries and print fairs. Her books travel far and wide and are used by artists and travellers, as well as notetakers who love using a work of art to record their thoughts and ideas or by producing an illustrated visual diary.

Suzi says that there is something very special about creating a book by hand. It bypasses mass production and uses handprinted papers and simple tools, bringing new life as well as purpose to her printed works. Each book she creates is unique and incorporates a different cover design, paper insert and construction. Although book-making requires precision, she says that maintaining a handmade approach is important to her as it furthers the distinctiveness of the finished book.

Simple stitched books are a great way of repurposing print offcuts and seconds.

Project: Making a pamphlet stitch notebook

Swap your tablet for a hand-crafted journal in which you can record your holiday highlights or document your latest silkscreen printing breakthrough.

Suzi explains how to make a simple three-hole A5 pamphlet stitch notebook with 22 pages and incorporating a silkscreen print cover. This is one of the easiest ways of binding paper together using a print offcut as a cover and creating a new use for discarded artwork.

Try to use prints that are on heavy paper for durability, work in good light and always use a metal ruler and sharp scalpel when cutting paper.

EQUIPMENT AND MATERIALS

Use A4 paper that is around 120gsm or you can use photocopier paper. You might, however, want to use something that has a specific colour or texture. You will also need an endpaper of the same weight, but a different colour. These interior papers are referred to as signatures in the book and printing trade.

* Bone folder
* Awl (for piercing the paper)
* Needle: a bookbinder's needle No. 18 is recommended as it is stronger and has a larger hole for the binding thread
* Bookbinding thread or embroidery thread waxed with beeswax
* Sharp scissors
* Cutting board and scalpel
* Metal ruler
* Flat weights
* Small bulldog clip
* Piece of corrugated cardboard
* 22 pieces of A4 paper (signature papers)
* A4 piece of paper for the endpapers
* A4-shaped print offcut
* Bookbinding thread or waxed embroidery thread (35cm)

Method

For this you should work on a cutting board in good light. Prepare all your materials before binding.

Folding 'on the grain'

Always fold your paper parallel with the grain (the direction the paper fibres align with one another); this will ensure that the folds are sharp and reduces any warping in the finished book. You can check this by gently bending the paper into a curl in both directions and feeling the resistance. The direction that bends more easily with the least resistance is the right direction to fold.

Cutting and trimming

Make sure all papers are aligned correctly when trimming and lay a heavy weight on top to keep them in place. Use the blade edge, not the point of the scalpel, to trim the paper, carefully cutting through the layers.

Paper template for hole punching

A paper template is then inserted in the folds of the middle of the book to indicate the stitching holes. This is created from an A4 sheet of paper that is folded in half along the paper horizontally and vertically before gate folding. The central fold contains three horizontal lines that converge in the middle, indicating the stitching points.

Stitching the booklet

You can easily make a cradle to hold the spine of your book using a piece of waste corrugated cardboard. Use the cradle to hold the book in place when piercing the pages with the awl. Simply rest the spine in one of the cardboard indentations.

Always pull the thread gently in the direction of the stitch to avoid ripping the paper and trim any overhanging edges before pressing the book overnight.

The paper template showing the three interior stitching points is placed in the centre of the signature papers before the holes are punctured.

Preparing the signature and endpapers

Assemble all your materials. If using embroidery thread pull it through a block of beeswax to reduce the friction on the paper when stitching.

Stack all the signature papers together prior to folding and trim off 3mm with a metal ruler and scalpel.

'Book' fold all the signature pages and the endpaper, pressing the folds with the bone folder. Nestle all the folded papers together.

Place the folded pages under a weight and leave overnight.

Fold the printed cover leaving a 3mm gap at one edge. Turn the cover over and do the same on the back.

This creates a spine or gap to fit the folded signatures and the endpaper.

Piercing holes and stitching

Place the folded signatures inside the cover and use the bone folder to press the pages together.

Make a cardboard cradle for the book spine by folding a long section of corrugated card. The book spine should fit snugly in the indentation.

Place the template inside the middle of the folded papers, endpaper and cover paper. Use the awl to pierce three holes through all the folded sections and push through into the cardboard cradle. Keep the awl upright when making the holes.

Remove the template and attach the pages together with a strong bulldog clip. You can reinforce the holes with the fat part of the needle, but don't go all the way through.

Thread the needle through the centre hole in the middle of the book, pull the thread through to the back of the cover, catch hold of the thread tail with your thumb and hold firmly in place in the middle of the book.

Bring the needle back through the cover to the inside using the bottom hole and gently but firmly pull the thread all the way through. Put the needle through the top hole and pull the thread all the way through to the back. This creates a long stitch in the middle of the signature pages. Keep hold of the tail while you do this to maintain a tight stitch.

Now for the tricky bit! Let go of the tail and take the needle back through the centre hole on the spine side and the signature pages to the centrefold. Keep the thread tight.

Tie the two tail ends of thread together using an overhand knot.

Trim the ends of the thread and tease out the threads to make a tassel.

Always use the whole of the blade when trimming, continuously slicing through the paper and card layers.

Trimming

Place the book flat on the cutting surface and trim the overhang edges of the cover and internal pages. Don't try to cut through all at once, keep a steady hand on the ruler and slice through the paper a bit at a time.

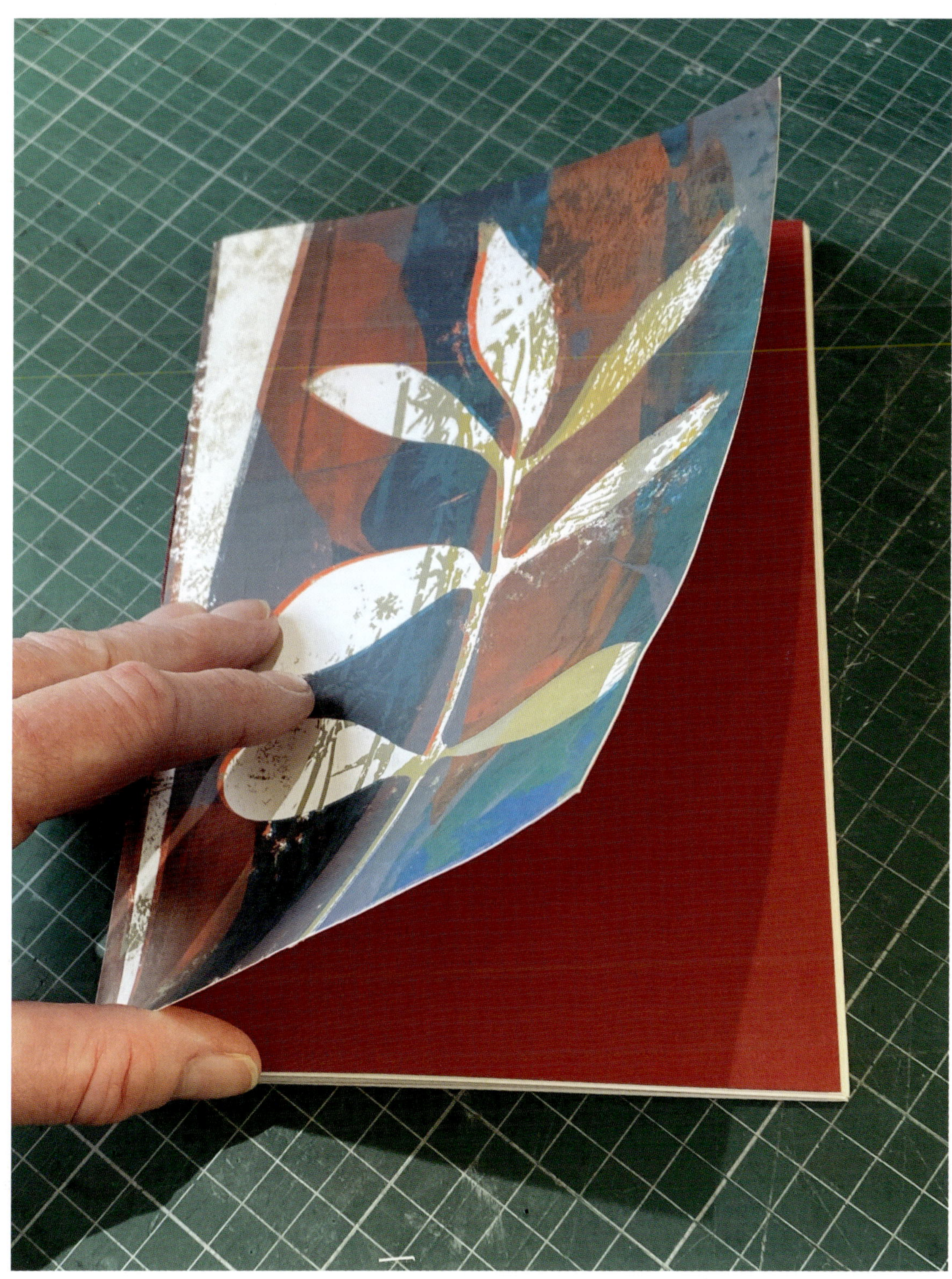

Silkscreen prints make great book covers. Try to keep cover paper weight at 300gsm.

PROJECT: CHRISTMAS PAPER STARS

This is a great way to use up misprints and produce a robust Christmas decoration and another chance to improve your paper folding. The three-dimensional star is created by making two folded stars and gluing them together.

Decorative paper stars with their own unique decoration.

MATERIALS AND EQUIPMENT

* 2 sheets of printed paper, cut into squares. Dimensions are dependent on size of paper
* Pair of scissors
* Pritt Stick
* Glue gun
* Hanging thread
* Pencil and ruler

Method

1 Prepare the paper shapes by cutting two paper squares the same size. 'Book' fold both squares on the horizontal. Fold both squares on the vertical and unfold.

2 'Shawl' fold both squares on both verticals and unfold.

3 Measure a quarter of the way up all four 'Book' folded lines and cut all four sides to the same length.

Turn the squares over on the wrong side and 'Kite' fold the four corners of each to create a star shape.

Glue one side of each 'Kite' fold and overlap the other fold to create four raised points of the star.

Take the two stars and stick the shapes together using a glue gun, offsetting the shapes to create an eight-pointed star.

PROJECT: GREETINGS CARDS

The best way to approach making your own greetings cards is to buy pre-cut cards with envelopes. You can print on both sides as well as make multicoloured prints. Cards can be printed edge to edge, where the design flows over the edge of the card, or you can maintain a border. Cards don't take up much space so you can print large numbers quite quickly.

Cards are a popular sales choice too, so you might consider keeping your screen for future use.

Method

Select your blank cards carefully and make sure they have envelopes. This project uses cards that are A5 when folded. Your design should fit within the card area as there is no trimming. You may find difficulty printing if your design stretches to the edges of the paper, so make room for paper handling when printing.

Making the stencils

My Christmas card used two colours (black and white). The design was laid out in landscape orientation on florists' acetate. Both stencils were hand-painted with elements of collage. I added a texture to both stencils by scratching into the ink when it was dry.

Printing

The white stencil was printed first and the black stencil overprinted. I also included a credit for the back of the card. This was output from my computer on acetate and pasted onto the black stencil.

When printing onto pre-cut cards make sure that you leave print-handling room at the bottom edges.

EQUIPMENT AND MATERIALS

This project will use two photographic stencils painted or drawn onto film. It will be a two-colour print. If you wish, the design might run across the front and back of the card and incorporate artist information or any other credits.

It's also possible to use paper stencils and the filler technique to print on cards, and you can also use a digital program to create the stencils.

* Screen (90–120 mesh)
* Squeegee
* Masking tape
* Photo stencil-making equipment
* Printing ink and printing binder
* Pre-cut greetings cards with envelopes (minimum 300gsm)
* Ruler
* Stencil films (cellophane, Maylar, etc.)
* Indian ink and acrylic pens for drawing onto film
* Paper or filler materials for analogue stencils

Both stencils were created by hand using Indian ink and collage.

Choose different coloured cards to produce a different range of prints.

PROFILE: ZOË EADY

glassgarden.co.uk

Zoë Eady is a glass artist based in Leeds. Her studio, The Glass Garden, can be found in the Spinning Mill in Farsley's Sunny Bank Mills, where she creates her stained glass artwork using both traditional and modern techniques.

Zoë Eady in her studio.

Zoë is a multimedia artist who combines analogue and digital in her creative process. She has had a studio at Sunnybank Mills in Leeds for more than ten years where she works on stained-glass commissions and creates three-dimensional structures in wood. Primarily a stained-glass artist, Zoë has moved into other media including lino printing and wood engraving. She also makes a range of decorative wooden models with silkscreen printed designs.

Zoë has recently transferred her lino images onto stained glass via the silkscreen process using high-quality transparencies of the original artwork. The black glass paint is screened in the usual way prior to firing using a photo stencil of her original design.

Although Zoë is proficient in digital design, she explains that doing everything digitally makes her work look lifeless and flat: 'The trick is to find a balance and use it as a tool and not a medium.' Zoë has managed to strike that balance by reusing the paper stencils she has used to make her silkscreen prints and by turning her handmade lino prints into digital motifs.

By scanning her designs into Adobe Illustrator, she has used the 'Image Trace' tool to outline her scanned images and create motifs that maintain their hand-cut origins. These motifs are vector images, and she can scale them to any size without loss of quality.

An example of Zoë's silkscreen printed glass.

PRINTING ON WOOD

When printing on wood the main consideration is that the surface needs to be smooth. You also need to place the printed objects in a wooden jig to maintain registration and protect the screen from any sharp edges during printing. You can also print without a jig, but in that case you will need to smooth all the cut edges. This works better on large surfaces and is not recommended for small objects.

Zoë laser cuts her wooden shapes and keeps them in their surround during printing. Zoë uses both paper and photo stencils to make her prints.

Acrylic ink can be used with a paper binder. Always use a spray varnish to protect the surface from scratching after printing. Print as if printing on paper and ensure you have a good snap to avoid smudging. The film method of registration works best when printing on wood.

Zoë's wooden motifs are double sided and she has created a mirror-image stencil to print on the back. The jig and printed shapes are kept in position, flipped over when dry and printed on the reverse side. The printed motifs are then popped out of their wooden encasement.

Zoë's hand-cut paper stencils are scanned into her computer and turned into vector designs, which she uses to laser cut her wooden decorations and output her silkscreen stencils.

The Maylar method of registration is used to align the design on top of the wooden shapes.

A wooden jig, made from a thin piece of MDF secured to the printing table base, carries the wooden printing surface.

PRINTING ON TEXTILES

Silkscreen printing onto fabric is an easy and accessible way to decorate pre-made T-shirts and bags as well as lengths of plain cloth for items such as wall hangings, lampshades and home furnishings. However, you may need to experiment with ink consistency and screen mesh to get the best results as textiles come in many different weights and surface textures.

Fabric is very absorbent, too, and requires a heavier ink deposit than paper.

Simple bold designs work best as lots of design details such as halftones and text are difficult to print. Paper, filler and photo stencils can all be used to print the design. You will also need to consider what you are going to turn the fabric into. If you are planning to cover a tablecloth or blinds, for example, you may want a repeat pattern.

EQUIPMENT AND MATERIALS

Textile printing requires a more open printing mesh weave, and I recommend a 43T mesh count. Natural fabrics such as cotton or linen work best and need to be heat set with an iron. You can also silkscreen print using textile dyes instead of fabric paint, which you will need to fix after the printing process.

Screens are manhandled into position: you don't need to use the printing baseboard. It's best to ask a friend to hold the screen down and generally help with the printing process.

* Printing fabric prepared for printing and ironed
* Padded printing board
* Screen (43-mesh count)
* Squeegee
* Printing inks and binder
* Iron to heat-fix ink and greaseproof paper
* Paper stencils or photo stencils

Tote bag with lobster design.

Create a textile printing base by layering flat lengths of materials such as fabric and rubber underlay. Stretch them across the edge of the table with heavy-duty clips.

Method

The following method describes the acrylic fabric ink process. The printed example uses one colour on a medium-weight calico tote bag, which is ironed to fix the surface ink.

Creating a textile printing base

Make a fabric printing pad by covering a piece of wood with an old woollen blanket or stretch a couple of blankets across a table and secure with clamps. This will be your printing base, and the printing fabric and screen will sit on top. There is no gap between the screen and fabric as they need to be in close contact during the printing process.

Ink

You need a specialised acrylic textile printing ink, or you can use a textile binder to mix your own colours. Make sure that the ink is a thick consistency, otherwise it may bleed into the fabric.

Design

Consider how big your design needs to be and where it's going to fit on the fabric. Here I have made an A3 photo stencil that fits my bag but avoids the handle stitching. I have placed it in the middle of the screen with plenty of room around the edges.

Stencils and screens

Paper stencils can also be used and cut as in previous chapters. I have used a 43-mesh screen that accommodates the design but isn't too big for the printing area. Screens are positioned over the material in close contact, and you can either weigh them down or get someone to do this for you during the printing process.

Registration

See the three steps below.

If you are printing on a T-shirt or bag, slip a piece of paper between to prevent the ink staining the backs.

Place the tote bag on the printing base and attach the stencil on top with masking tape where you want it to print. Tape a border around the fabric bag. This is the print position of all the bags.

Leave the bag in position, place the screen on top and match up the stencils. Tape the outside edges of the screen with contrasting tape to define the screen position. Remove the screen.

Printing

Place the screen on top of the bag in the printing position. Load the screen with ink and get help to hold the frame in position. Flood the screen with ink while in contact with the fabric and print. Remove the screen carefully and place the textile on a washing line to dry. If using a T-shirt or similar, remove the paper insert as soon as possible otherwise it may stick to the fabric. You may have to flood and print several times to get a strong print.

When the print has dried, iron it to fix on both sides, using a piece of greaseproof paper between the iron and the fabric.

Insert the bag into the printing position.

Place the screen on top of the bag in the printing position. Load the screen with ink. You may need help to hold the frame in position. Flood the screen with ink while in contact with the fabric and print.

Remove the screen carefully and place the textile on a washing line to dry. If using a T-shirt or similar remove the paper insert as soon as possible otherwise it may stick to the fabric. You may have to flood and print several times to get a strong print.

ROFILE: LILY KELLETT

Lily Kellett working on her kitchen table.

wayfaringwild.com
Lily Kellett is the printmaker behind Wayfaring Wild. Based in North Yorkshire, Lily makes linocut prints that are inspired by the landscape of her home and family life around the kitchen table.

Lily Kellett is a creative practitioner who designs and makes simple linocut prints that she undertakes on her kitchen table. Observational drawing has always been part of her creative practice, and she is inspired by her rural surroundings, drawing on plants and still life to create simple and bold prints. Her recent prints feature seasonal food.

Lino was a great way for her to start with print and she borrowed tools from her grandparents, who were both professional printmakers. Lily is largely self-taught and the new skills she learned gave her the confidence to set up a small online print business, which has enabled her to combine working from home and caring for her young daughter.

Lily creates coloured backgrounds for her prints using the reduction print technique and she has been keen to learn how to utilise simple silkscreen printing techniques to achieve this on her kitchen table.

The step by step approach given below describes how she creates a silkscreen printed background for one of her food-inspired prints. This process utilises simple paper-cut stencils and a basic print set-up that easily fits on a kitchen table. You will also need access to water and somewhere to dry prints. Lily mixed her acrylic inks with ink binder to the desired colours and printed on handmade Japanese printing paper. These were left to dry prior to applying the lino print.

COMBINING SILKSCREEN WITH LINO AND WOODCUT

Method

Lily chose one of her artichoke lino prints to combine with a silkscreen backdrop. She set up all her equipment and materials on the kitchen table and carefully masked off a screen and mixed inks.

Stencil making
She cut out a paper stencil that matched her artichoke lino print to make the background; this contained some fine white lines. Freezer paper was used for the stencil as the design had delicate paper bridges.

Registration
Using the paper pick-up method of printing, she first printed on a piece of Maylar to line up the registration on the printing paper with the original background lino print.

Silkscreen printing
She used a thin Japanese printing paper and printed a blend of green by mixing the colours on the screen. Although the printing paper was thin, the paper fibres were very strong and the surface remained flat.

EQUIPMENT AND MATERIALS

* Printing board
* Screen (90 mesh)
* Squeegee
* Scalpel
* Cutting board
* Palette knives
* Ink and printing binder
* Stencil paper
* Printing paper suitable for lino
* Masking tape
* Sheet of Maylar

Lino printing

When the under-colour had dried, she inked up her linocut in a dark contrasting green, placed it in a jig and lined up her paper.

The lino print was successfully transferred on top of the silkscreen print.

Setting up the screen in the kitchen demonstrates the accessibility of the process.

Registration using a Maylar sheet.

Background blended print.

Registering the background print with the linocut.

The completed print combining silkscreen and lino.

EDITIONING AND FINISHING

Remember that all your prints are created by your own hand. Ink is pulled through the mesh with a squeegee and each print is unique because of the process. Limited-edition prints are exactly as described: 'Limited', no more, no less. They are also described as identical, although with all handmade printing processes there are always variations in colour and reproduction.

When I make a limited-edition print, I do not reprint the edition. When the edition is gone, it's gone! Occasionally I do not print a large edition in one go as I don't have the room in my studio or plan chest. For example, I might print 25 out of an edition of 50, accepting that there might be a slight colour variation in printing the subsequent 25.

I should add a note of warning about taking care when numbering an edition, as I recently saw a large woodcut print at auction of which I have a copy with the same edition number!

Placing an identification mark on your work is proof of creative origin. The practice of signing and editioning handmade prints comes when you are feeling confident enough to create a limited printed number of the same design. There are also a range of specific editioning variations relating to monotype or monoprints, print proofs, open editions and so on.

You don't have to edition your work as a simple signature will do, so I don't think you need to be pressurised into following the guidelines described in this chapter. For example, when I make large runs of greetings cards, which I don't sign by hand as I may repeat the run, I tend to print a text credit and incorporate it in the design.

We are now at the end of the printing process and the start of the 'finishing'. It is a chance to check the quality of your prints, set aside any that have misregistration or inky thumb prints on the paper edge, and assemble your best work. Remember that you are creating handmade works of art and an inky thumb print on the back of a print or on the outer edge is proof of this.

Remember, you are not discarding those prints you deem to have not made the final cut as you can incorporate them in other artwork, print over them or sell them as seconds.

Trimming

Before you start putting pencil to paper, once the ink has dried on your prints you need to think about cutting and trimming. I usually make my prints with a border so I can remove any inky marks on the edge by trimming. If I'm trimming handmade paper, I use a folding/scoring and tearing method to maintain the deckled edge of the paper. On thick card or paper, I tend to use a rotary guillotine.

If I am trying to retain the deckled edge of handmade paper I simply lay a heavy metal ruler where I want the edge to be, run a wet brush along the edge and leave it for a few seconds, press down on the ruler and tear off the paper. Be careful not to overwet the paper.

Editioning process

You can edition a print that uses just one colour or a complex multicoloured design using lots of different screens. Bear in mind that the more colours you use in a print the longer it will take to produce a print run.

Edition size

Give some thought to how many prints you are going to produce, what paper you are going to use, its size and so on. I still commonly produce small editions of 10 to 25 prints as I have a small studio, and I hang my work from a washing line. Print collectors tend to value prints from small editions and this can increase their value.

Test prints

I always include a few extra prints that I use at the start of each colour run to test the colours and registration. These are my proof prints and I make them on less expensive paper. Occasionally I will test print a whole print using proofs to evaluate the design, colour and other qualities and decide on the size of the edition on this basis. This can be very time consuming but is necessary before committing to expensive handmade paper.

Limited-edition prints: Numbering and signing

Line up all the prints that you want to include in the edition. Remove any test prints or proofs. I use an HB pencil to sign my work in the bottom right-hand corner of the print, followed by the date. I try to keep the signature in line with the print edges. I write the edition number as a fraction in the bottom left-hand corner of the print, for example, 1/20, 2/20 and so on.

All my limited-edition prints have titles, which I write centrally under the print enclosed within single quotation marks, as in 'The Grape Pickers'.

To ensure that all my editioning marks line up exactly on each print, I create a paper template that I position under each print and use as a visual marker.

Try to keep your handwriting consistent and pay particular attention to your signature, as variation can cause confusion.

Edition categories: Variations

Varied or Variable Edition (VE or EV)

There is lots to think about when considering editioning prints that have variations, but similar content. If you make a print that combines paper stencils, screen painting and a top photo stencil, for example, there may only be variations in the under-printing. Therefore, these prints should be considered variable. Editions that contain prints made using these variations should be signed (VE) followed by the number in the edition in the bottom left-hand corner. The use of a different printing paper in the edition is also often labelled with this abbreviation.

Trial Proof (T/P)

Prints made during the process of adjusting and developing. I don't use this abbreviation in my printing process, although many artists do.

Artist's Proofs (A/P)

Artist's proofs should be signed A/P in the bottom left-hand corner; no numbering system is used. As discussed, an 'Artist's Proof' is the same as other prints within the edition but may have colour variations or be printed on less expensive paper. Proofs are still desirable, mostly because they are part of the artist's 'workings out'.

Unique Prints (1/1)

Monoprints or prints with lots of variations should be classed as 'unique print' or marked 1/1 in the left-hand corner and signed and dated to the left. I always include a title too. Alternatively, you can apply MP or MT.

Open Editions (O/E)

These are prints that are not limited to a specific number of prints and are considered less valuable by collectors. Open edition silkscreen prints use the same stencils for creating repeat prints. You can remove the stencil from a screen and repeat the stencil-making process later.

Print storage

Once you have finished editioning your prints, carefully store them somewhere flat and dry. They can be placed on top of one another without the need for tissue paper, although I prefer to store my prints with acid-free tissue between the sheets. I place them in number order and keep a record of how many I have sold. If you are preparing to sell them at an event, then wrap them in cellophane with a card backing to protect them from handling and make them easy to view.

Stencil storage

I find this just as important as print storage. If you decide to repeat an edition, or if you didn't print all your edition in one go and need to remake the stencil for a specific print, it can be infuriating to find a scrunched-up acetate at the bottom of the plan chest. Take care of your handmake stencils by placing them in paper folders with titles. Make sure you include all the colour breakdown stencils too. Don't be tempted to roll the films as you will find that mark-making materials such as ink and paint will part company.

SUPPLIERS

Screen Ink & Solvent Supplies Ltd
Unit 3, Rugby Park,
Battersea Rd,
Stockport SK4 3EB
www.inkandsolvents.co.uk
Screens, inks and emulsions. Screen recovering service.

Handprinted Ltd
22 Arun Business Park,
Shripney Road,
Bognor Regis PO22 9SX
www.handprinted.co.uk
Silkscreen kits, screens, emulsion, recovering service. General art materials including printing paper. Technical blog featuring silkscreen process.

Turners Graphic Art and Drawing Office Supplies Ltd
Integrity House, Lumsdale Road,
Lower Lumsdale, Matlock,
Derbyshire DE4 5EX
www.turnersart.co.uk
General art materials, silkscreen equipment, ink and emulsion. Supplies Mark Resist film, ink. Supplies inkjet and laser stencil films.

John Purcell Paper
15 Rumsey Road,
London SW9 0TR
www.johnpurcell.net
Extensive paper range. Stocks print and bookmaking papers and True-Grain film.

Ideal Stencils
Unit 8, Driffield Business Centre,
Scotchburn Garth,
Driffield YO25 6EF
www.idealstencils.co.uk
Stocks Maylar on rolls.

Shepherds Bookbinders Ltd
30 Gillingham Street,
London SW1V 1HU
store.bookbinding.co.uk
Bookbinding materials and equipment, including fine art papers, threads, needles and so on.

Jackson's Art Supplies
1 Farleigh Place,
London N17 7SX
www.jacksonsart.com
General art materials.

Seawhite of Brighton Ltd
Star Road Trading Estate,
Brighton,
West Sussex RH13 8RY
www.seawhite.co.uk
Paper and general art materials.

Wicked Printing Stuff
Screen Ink and Solvent Supplies Ltd
Unit 3, Rugby Park,
Battersea Road, Stockport,
Cheshire SK4 3EB
www.wickedprintingstuff.com
Screen printing supplies, inks, emulsions and stencil films

INDEX

First published in 2025 by
The Crowood Press Ltd
Ramsbury, Marlborough
Wiltshire SN8 2HR

enquiries@crowood.com
www.crowood.com

British Library Cataloguing-in-Publication Data
A catalogue record for this book is available from the British Library.

For product safety-related questions, contact:
productsafety@crowood.com

ISBN 978 0 7198 4575 8

Typeset by Envisage IT

Cover design by Sergey Tsvetkov

Printed and bound in India by Nutech Printing Services

Acknowledgements

I would like to say a big thank you to all my family and friends and the wider printmaking community for their support and technical help in the production of this book. Special thanks to everyone who took part in testing out the many creative and practical activities and giving honest feedback throughout.

I would like to give particular thanks to Kim Coley for her assistance, being the perfect hand model and reading my drafts. I am also extremely grateful to Eric Moss for helping to capture and describe each chapter with his original photographic flair.

I would like to acknowledge the many artists and printmakers whose creativity has inspired me. This handbook is a testament to the power of collaboration and community. I would like to give specific thanks to fellow Yorkshire printmakers James Bywood and Nikki Williams for providing an insight into their digital techniques, inviting me into their home studios and sharing their personal printmaking stories.

I am also extremely appreciative to Lily Kellett for setting up a print space in her kitchen and exploring lino and silkscreen printing, Suzi Thompson for showing me simple bookbinding and Zoë Eady for sharing her methods of printing onto wood.

Lastly, a special thank you to my husband Richard, whose support has been constant from beginning to end.